ETHNIC CHRONOLOGY SERIES
NUMBER 31

The Arabs
in America
1492-1977
A Chronology & Fact Book

Compiled and edited by

Beverlee Turner Mehdi

1978
OCEANA PUBLICATIONS, INC.
DOBBS FERRY, NEW YORK

Library of Congress Cataloging in Publication Data

Mehdi, Beverlee Turner, 1930-
   The Arabs in America, 1492-1977.

   (Ethnic chronology series; no. 31)
   Bibliography: p.
   Includes index.
   SUMMARY: A history of Arabs in the United States
with illustrative documents, appendices, and bibliography.
   1. Arab Americans—History—Chronology.
2. Arab Americans—History-Sources. [1. Arab
Americans—History] I. Title II. Series.
E184.A65M44   973'.04'927   77-27463
ISBN 0-379-00527-1

To the memory of
Rev. William Henry Turner
and
Al-Haj Mohammed Abdullah Mehdi

TABLE OF CONTENTS

EDITOR'S FOREWORD

When we speak of Arab-Americans, we are, in reality, speaking of a group of Americans who trace their heritage to some twenty different Arab countries, extending from Morocco in the West to the United Arab Emirates in the East. As would be expected, a geographical area this large has not produced a single homogenous culture, but rathter has been a melting pot for cultures differing in race, religion, and political ideology. What then is an Arab? An Arab is a person who comes from the part of the world described above, speaks the Arabic language, and considers himself or herself to be an Arab.

Thus, the problem of gathering information about Arab-Americans begins to become clear. From the fifteenth century to the end of World War I, that part of the Arab world which includes Syria, Lebanon, Palestine, Jordan, Iraq, much of the Arabian Penninsula and much of North Africa was ruled by Turkey, then known as the Ottoman Empire. Persons emigrating to the United States from those areas were frequently classified as "Turks." Those who were not classified as Turks were classified as Syrians. It is important to remember that historically, "Greater Syria" included Syria, Lebanon, Palestine, Jordan, and occasionally Iraq. Throughout this book the reader will often find the classification Syrian-American used instead of Arab-American.

Emigration from the Arab world to the United States began in earnest in 1886 and reached a peak in 1914. These early immigrants were primarily Christians. It is frequently surprising to Americans to learn that there are over 9,000,000 Arabs who are Christian. Their life had been primarily one of neglect, as life had been for most of the Ottoman's subjects.

Throughout the Middle East at this time there was only a rudimentary feeling of nationhood. A person's loyalty was first to his family and then to his religious group and village. Frequently, villages were comprised almost entirely of one religious group. In Syria (including Lebanon) from which the early emigration to America took place, the Christians were divided into three major groups: Syrian Orthodox, Maronite, and Melkite.

These three groups could trace their ancestry to Christianity's earliest days in the actual countryside where it began. By the end of the nineteenth century, and the beginning of the period of emigration with which we are concerned, the Maronites and Melkites were in communion with the Church in Rome (Roman Catholic) while maintaining their own rites. The Syrian Orthodox, on the other hand, continued to follow the Byzantine Rite and were not in communion with Rome.

The Moslems in the area had their own major divisions into Sunni, Shiah, and Druze. Because the Ottoman rulers were themselves Moslem, the Syrian Moslems did not suffer the same discrimination which the Syrian Christians suffered. When one element of discrimination was eliminated, however, and the Syrian Christians were conscripted into the army, as the Moslems always had been, many of the Christians decided to emigrate.

Another factor which gave rise to emigration was the contact the Syrian Christians had with the American Christian Missionaries. As the American Christians had very little success in proselytizing, they turned their attention to providing services for the area. They built hospitals and schools and manned these institutions with such commitment and selflessness that it made a profound impression upon the Syrians and caused them to generalize as to what the character of Americans must be like.

The "Early Immigration Period" of Arab-Americans was a period roughly from 1885 to 1914 when the majority of immigrants were Syrian Christians who were poor, uneducated, and anxious to leave an area where Ottoman rule and religious factionalism produced bloody upheavals. The importance of the Syrians' heritage as the great traders and merchants of the Mediterranean must not be overlooked. This legacy from the time of the Phoenicians made them accepting of the idea of travel and relocation, and their business sense of trade and hard work gave them confidence as they looked toward a new land of opportunity.

By 1914, 106,721 Syrians had arrived in the United States. Their lack of knowledge of the English language and their distaste for indoor factory environments caused the vast majority of these immigrants to become peddlars of wares door-to-door. Peddling was an honorable profession in the Middle East, and although it was not looked upon favorably by the more established, urban Americans, they were welcome guests out in the countryside. They sold not only much-needed essentials, needles, thread, shoelaces and notions of all kinds for rural families, but they also brought a change in the day's routine. Often, they were welcomed by hospitable farm people to share a meal and frequently asked to spend the night if the hour were late.

In this way the peddlar perfected his English, learned about America and Americans, and, in many cases, made sufficient money to settle in an area and open a small store. Once settled, he proceeded to bring over his relatives and establish a church.

During the years betreen the two world wars, immigration from the Arab world, as well as many other areas, dwindled to a trickle as restrictive immigration laws were passed by the United States Congress.

The "Later Immigration Period" began in 1945. The Arab world immigrants during this period were quite different form those of the early period. These newcomers were in large part professionals and well-educated (many of them in American universities). A large percentage were Moslem. They came not only from Syria and Lebanon, but also from Egypt, Iraq, and Palestine. They are what has been referred to as the "brain drain" immigrants, - the M.D.'s and Ph.D.'s They are more politically aware and active and much more willing to call themselves Arabs, rather than Syrians, Lebanese, Egyptians, etc.

The creation of the state of Israel and later the defeat in the 1967 war, while humiliating, acted as catalysts toward the self-identification of Syrian-Americans; After 1973, the new power and prestige which oil wealth bestowed upon them added a pride in being Arab-American can.

While as an ethnic group in the United States today, their number is small - one and one-half million - and because they have so easily assimilated, many Americans are unaware of the Arab-American existence. They do exist, however, and as in the case of the recent Ralph Nader slur, they are standing up to be counted and letting their voices be heard. It is a good thing, too, for in the last half of the twentieth century the Arab world may be the important unknown in any equation dealing with international destinies. In this case, the Arab-American may well help provide the balance in such an equation.

Beverlee Turner Mehdi
College at Old Westbury
Old Westbury, New York

THE PERIOD BEFORE 1885

480 B.C.-
146 B.C.
In his book, <u>They All Discovered America</u>, Charles Michael Boland stated that he believed the Phoenicians
(people of the land today known as Lebanon) to have
been in America during this period. He cites hewn
stones and inscriptions found near North Salem, New
Hampshire (Pattee's Caves) and in southern Pennsylvania near Mechanicsburg. It is his theory that the Pheo-
nicians , the most renowned traders of the period, were
were blown off course during trips to Ultima Thule
(Iceland) and were sent scudding down to New England.
Joseph Ayoob of Alquippa, Pennsylvania has also written on this theory in his tract, "Were the Phoenicians
the First to Discover America?"

PRE 1492
According to the Arab geographer al-Sherif al-Idrisi
eight adventurous Arabs had sailed from Lisbon, Por-
tugal, trying to discover what was beyond the "Sea of
Darkness," the Arab name for the Atlantic. It is said
that they landed in South America. Historians deny
that this report by al-Idrise inspired Columbus to try
to reach the East by sailing west, leading to the great
discovery of America. But in 1955, when Italy celebrated the five-hundredth year of Columbus' birth, there
was a fair at which many of his belongings were dis-
played. Included in this collection was an Arabic book,
said to be the first Idrisi book, in which the author
mentioned the story of the eight Arab adventurers.

1492
It is reported that Columbus took with him Louis de
Torre to act as his Arabic interpreter when his expected meeting took place with the Grand Khan of India.
Torre was a Spanish-Arab who acquired his Spanish name
when he converted to Christianity at the end of the
700 year-long Arab Moorish presence in Granada.

1539
A certain Estephan (Istifan), a Moroccan Arab, acted
as a guide to Fra Marcos de Nize, a Francescan sent by
the Viceroy of New Spain to lead an expedition into
the south-western part of North America. These areas,
today known as New Mexico and Arizona, were explored by
De Niza and Estephan. They entered areas where white
men had not been seen. Estephan, it is told, fell vic-
tim to a hostile Indian's arrow.

1668
Father Elias al-Mawsili of Mosul, Iraq, made an exten-
ded trip through Mexico and parts of Central and South
America. He recorded these travels in Arabic in <u>Rih-
lat Awwal Sharqi Ila Amrika</u> (The Trip of the First
Eastener to America).

1717
Arabic-speaking slaves arrived in the United States.
Words such as "Allah" and "Mohammed" and their refusal

to eat pork often identified men with names like Omar
Ibn Said, Job Ben Solomon, Paul Lahman Kibby, Prince
Omar, and Ben Ali.

1777   In a French document, dated December 20, 1777, Morocco
gave "de facto" recognition to the newly-declared independent United States of America and granted free
passage to all American ships. This document, signed
by Mohammed III, Emperor of Morocco, was circulated
to the Consuls and merchants in Tangiers.

1779   During the American Revolution the Continental Congress is said to have negotiated with Algeria to import horses for Washington's army. A ship bearing the
horses foundered off Cape Hattera and some of the men
and horses swam to shore. Oral tradition cites one
prominent American family of North Carolina as tracing
their ancestry to this incident.

1787   Morocco officially recognized the independence of the
United States thus making it the first county in the
world to do so. Mahammed III signed a "Treaty of
Friendship and Cooperation" with George Washington,
America's first President. The treaty was negotiated
by the first American Ambassador to Morocco, Mr.
Barclay in 1786 and signed by the King of Morocco on
June 23, 1786. After ratification by the United States
Congress on July 18, 1787, a letter of thanks was
sent to King Mohammad III. The letter asked the King
to use his good offices as a mediator between the United States and the rulers of Tunisia and Tripoli at
that time. The Moroccan mediation effort was successful.
                    (See document No. 1)

1790   The House of Representatives in South Carolina provided that "sundry Moors, Subjects of the Emperor of Morocco," be tried in court according to the laws for
South Carolina citizens and not under Negro codes.

1840   Sayyid Said Bin Sultan, Ruler of Muscat, Zanzihar and
Their Dependencies, (today known as Muscat and Oman)
sent the bark al-Sultanah to deliver the first cargo
load of goods on an Omani ship under the 1834 trade
treaty ratified by Sayyid Said and the United States
government. The arrival in New York harbor of the
Sultanah, its commander, Al-Haj Ahmad Bin Na'aman,
and crew provided a great deal of excitement for New
Yorkers who welcomed and feted these newcomers during
their three month stay. The newspapers carried fre-
quetn accounts of the Sultana's visit and a portrait

of Ahmad bin Naaman hangs in the offices of the Art
Commission in New York City Hall.

(See document No. 2)

1848   Father Flavianus Kfoury, a Melkite Catholic priest,
came to the United States to collect donations to help
rebuild St. John's Convent in Khonchara, Lebanon. He
spent two years in the United States, traveling to New
York, Philadelphia, Rochester, Birmingham, Charleston
and other cities carrying with him letters of introduction from Bishop John Hughes, Bishop of New York. In
one of his letters Bishop Hughes stressed the importance of assisting the Syrian priest since he was "the
first of the Greek Catholic Rite" to be referred to
them.

(See document No. 3)

1854   Antonio Bishallany, a young Syrian who had become acquainted with the Christian missionaries in the Near
East came at their suggestion to study at the Amenia
Seminary in New York. It was his plan to complete his
education and then return to minister to his own people. Unfortunately, he contracted tuberculosis and
died within two years. His grave is in the Greenwood
Cemetary in Brooklyn, New York.

(See documents No. 4 and No. 5)

1855   Gregory Wortabet, an American whose family had long
been residents in Beirut, came to America and shortly afterwards, returned to Syria. Wortabet was an
educated assistant to the American missionaries in
Beirut.

1856   May 14. At Indianola, Texas, a ship arrived from the
Near East with a cargo of thirty-three camels, which
had been contracted for by the United States government.
With the camels came two Turks and three Arabs who were
highly qualified in the handling of the animals. One
of these Arabs became well-known in the southwestern
United States by the nickname "Hadgi Ali" which later
became "Hi Jolly".

(See documents No. 6, No. 7, and No. 11)

1857   An additional forty-four camels were imported to add
to those already serving the United States Army in
the Southwest.

1860's A Mr. Antonius Yanni of Tripoli, Syria, who was a strong
supporter of the Union cause in the American Civil War,
sent two boxes filled with cones of cedar, seashells,
and other Syrian curios to the United States to benefit
the Union cause. A church in Worcester, Massachusetts

sold the items and used the money to buy 720 New
Testaments for the boys in blue.

1864   Sahle Sabrinji, from Syria, came to the United States,
            at the request of Dr. Cornelius Van Dyck of the Pres-
            byterian Board of Missions, to assist in reading proofs
            of the new Arabic translation of the Bible.

1869   The opening of the Suez Canal played a large part in
            the emigration of Arabs from Yemen to the United States.
            Most came through the port of New York and then made
            their way west to cities such as Buffalo and Detroit.
            It is well known that a number of Yemeni sailors jump-
            ed ship in San Francisco and settled down to life on
            the West Coast.

1870   The Homestead Act of 1862 became known in the Arab
            countries by 1870 and rumor had it that the "malak"
            (king) was giving away land in the United States.
            Numerous farmers from the mountainous areas of Leba-
            non and Syria left their homeland, lured by the idea
            of free farm land. B'sherreh (Bisha 'lah), the home
            village of Kahlil Gibran, reportedly sent some of her
            sons to acquire such lands.

1875   New Orleans, Louisiana, served as an active port of
            entry to the United States for immigrants from the Arab
            lands. It provided easy access to travel both north-
            ward and westward, and by this date the immigrant found
            "Lebanese hotels" in the city awaiting him.

1876   The Centennial Exposition held in Philadelphia attract-
            ed merchants from throughout the Arab world. These
            merchants brought with them the perfume of atter of re-
            ses, olive wood carvings, gold filagree jewels, amber
            beads, ceramic vases and rosaries. The religious items
            from Palsestine, and especially those from Jerusalem
            sold so well that a number of these Arab merchants sent
            home for more. They peddled these items throughout the
            area, and many stayed on to set up import centers for
            other peddlers and to become American citizens.

1877   Seven Algerians, who claimed to be escaped military
            prisoners from French Guiana, arrived in New York City
            by way of Wilmington, North Carolina.
                        (See document No. 8)

1878   The family of Dr. Joseph (Yusef) Arbeely emigrated from
            Damascus to the United States. This was a highly edu-
            cated family, the father having been the president at
            the Patriarchal Syrian College of the Greek Church in
            his native city. This was a family that immigrated

with the goal of settling permanently in the United
States, whereas other immigrants during this period
had come merely to make their fortunes and then return
to the old country. Two of Dr. Arbeely's sons founded
the first Arabic newspaper in the United States, Kow-
kab Amerika (The Star of America).
(See document No. 9)

1880's   Emmigrants from Zahleh, Syria went westward to the
                large cities where they engaged in trading. They began
                by peddling but remained to found businesses in the
                northern cities from Buffalo, New York, to Duluth, Min-
                nesota.

1881   Feb. 22. An official presentation was made of "Cleo-
                patra's Needle" the obelisk which was the gift of the
                Khedive of Egypt to the City of New York. Henry Hurl-
                burt, editor of the New York World was an ardent advo-
                cate of closer Egyptian-American relation. The story
                is told that when the Khedive asked Mr. Hurlburt, "Have
                you a particular obelisk in mind?" Mr. Hurlburt is said
                to have replied, "Forgive the pun, Your Highness - but
                any old obelisk will do." The one chosen had been
                quarried at Aswan in the 15th century B.C., weighed
                224 tons and was 69 feet 6 inches high. Its lovely
                hieroglyphics were shortly ravaged by New York's cor-
                rosive fumes, but the obelisk still stands in Central
                Park with the same orientation to the sun which it had
                in Egypt.

1882   The Arabi Pasha revolt in Egypt which caused Syrians to
                emigrate to America, rather than Egypt, made this year
                in reality the beginning of the large-scale Syrian move-
                ment to America.

1885   Religion was the main reason that fewer Moslems emi-
                grated from the Near East. The story is told of an
                elderly Moslem lady in Detroit who said, "In 1885,
                my father planned to accompany some Christian friends
                to America. He bought the ticket and boarded the boat.
                Shortly before sailing he asked the captain whether
                America had mosques. Told that it had none, he feared
                that America was bilad kufr (a land of unbelief). He
                immediately got off the boat."

                THE PERIOD OF THE EARLY IMMIGRATION

                           1885 - 1914

                The period of substantial emigration to America by peo-
                ple from the Arabic-speaking countries was from 1885-

1914. This period of "Early Immigration" was comprised for the most part of Arab Christians from what
is today known as Syria and Lebanon. These Arab Christians were divided into three major religious groupings:
Ortodox, Melkite, and Maronite and as there was no
concept of a national loyalty, the loyalty of each of
these immigrants was to his village and his religious
sect.
(See document No. 10)

1889
By this date, the Arab-American Melkite Catholic Community in New York had a visiting priest, Father Abraham Bashawatah, B.S., who for many years ministered to
the community having a juridcal permanent status.
It was not until 1915 that St. George's Parish, New
York City, was canonically erected.

1889
Trinity Church of New York City, in its February Record
stated, "There is within a quarter mile of the Parish
Church a community of Syrians, who, by every tie of
faith and apostolic descent and of humanity, are ours
to minister to and to succor."

1890's
The first Arab families settled in Manchester, New
Hampshire and in Springfield, Massachusetts. The
first settlers in Springlield came from Lebanon. The
migration which continued through the perid of the
First World War was a proletarian one, made up of
farmers, laborers, and small landowners. Many of the
immigrants were illiterate, having been totally neglected by the regime of the Ottoman rulers and outside the range of the Christian missions which operated mainly in the cities.

1891
Rev. Betrus Karkemoz arrived in New York from Syria to
become the first permanent Maronit clergyman in the
United States. By 1931, the Maronits had grown to
9,000 communicants and had thirty-four chuches.

1891
The Faour Shelala family opened the first Syrian Bank
in the United States at 63 Washington Street, in New
York City.

1892
Rev. Constantine Tirezi arrived in the United States
as the first Syrian Orthodox clergyman authorized by
the Antiochian patriarch to organize a church.
found the number of Greek Orthodoxs too small for a
church, and shortly returned to Syria. Up until the
year 1904 the Syrian Orthodox in America was under the
jurisdiction of the Russian Church of America whose
seat was in San Francisco.

1892   The first Arabic language newspaper in America began
       publication. It was titled Kawkab Amerika (The Star
       of America) and founded by Dr. Yusuf Arbeely's two
       sons, Dr. Ibrahim Arbeely and Najeeb Arbeely. The
       paper was produced weekly.

1893   The world-wide depression which affected international
       trade, reduced the demand for Syrian silk, caused its
       price to fall by one-half and encouraged the Syrian ex-
       odus to America.

1893   The World's Columbian Exposition in Chicago was publi-
       cized in newspapers of the Arab world. Merchants from
       many parts of the Middle East came to sell their wares,
       and the famed "Street of Cairo" on the Midway Plaisance
       drew much attention to that area. As was the case with
       the Philadelphia Centennial Exposition of 1876, many of
       those who came from the Arab world to sell their wares
       stayed on to settle. Consequently, a number of Arab-
       American families in the Great Lakes Region trace
       their origins to the Columbian Exposition.

1894   Musa Daoud, a fairly recent Arab immigrant, was the
       subject of a feature article in the New York Times of
       June 4th. It seems that Musa, a graduate of Catholic
       College in Beirut, had been searching out his fellow-
       countrymen when they arrived at Ellis Island and acted
       as their inerpreter. Daoud, who worked as a brick-
       layer and had a reputation as an honest man, was as
       strong as a Titan. He became the colony "leader" when
       he defended a peddlar in the area from attack. The
       place where he lived was open to newcomers. Daoud
       had, in fact, rebound old discarded boooks which proved
       valuable to the other tenants. The Times reporter was
       interested to see how Daoud and his friends spent
       their time in constant work and study.

1896   Dr. Joseph Arbeely's English Grammar was published
       as an aid to his countrymen who were struggling with
       the language.
         (See document No. 12)

1897   The newspaper Al Ayam (The Days) was published by Jo-
       seph Maloof in Arabic.

1898   Naoum Mokarzel began publication of the Arabic language
       newspaper, Al-Hoda (The Guidance). It began as a
       twice weekly publication, was later increased to five
       times a week, and then appeared only three times a
       week. Mokarzel used Al-Hoda to become undisputed
       leader of the Maronite Arab-Americans. The setting
       of Al-Hoda on an Arabic linotype machine in 1903

marked the first time this had ever been done in the
world of Arabic papers. Al-Hoda was begun in Philadelphia but moved to New York City in 1903.

1899   Paul Jabbour and his eldest daughter arrived in the
        United States from Sidon where he had been a licensed
        layman of the United Presbyterian Church. He served
        the Fall River, Massachussetts Syrian Community for
        many years as a lay preacher.

        Dr. Louis L. Williams, surgeon at the Marine Hospital
        in New York City reported that many Near Eastern im-
        migrants were arriving in the country with trachoma
        of the eyes. It was decreed that the steamship com-
        pany bringing the immigrants would have to pay for
        their medical treatment as this should have been check-
        ed before they left their homelands.

        The Arabic language newspaper Miraat Al-Gharb (The
        Mirror of the West) called by its readers Al-Miraat
        was founded in New York City by Najeeb Diab. Diab
        was an Orthodox Christian and Al-Miraat became the
        voice for the Orthodox Arab-American Community just
        as the Al-Hoda spoke for the Maronite Arab-Americans.
        (There were some bitter conflicts between these two
        papers reflecting their differing sectarian points of
        view).

        There was talk of a "Syrian Junta" rising in New York
        to activate Arab-Americans in a move against Abdul
        Hamid II. There was a good bit of soapbox oratory and
        much genuine enthusiasm for the idea of rising against
        the Ottoman Sultan, but distance proved too great a
        factor and the movement gradually waned.
                        (See document No. 13)

1900   The Syrian population of Manhattan and Brooklyn had
        grown past 10,000.

        The average amount of money per capita of Syrians
        entering the United States in this year was $14.31.

1901   United States Industrial Commission Report Vol. 15,
        page 36 stated, "the coming to the United States of
        a number of Syrians -- who are primarily peddlers of
        notions."
                        (See document No. 17)

1902   The family of Kaleel Hanna was the first to settle in
        Terre Haute, Indiana. Hanna and most of Terre Haute's
        Arab-Americans came from the village of Ein el-Charra,
        northwest of Damascus. They established a Syrian colony

in the area of North Fulton Street in this city on
the Wabash. Today Terre Haute's Arab-Americans number are more than 700 and they are proud to be the national headquarters for Project Ryaiat (Loving Care),
a humanitarian effort aimed at easing the suffering
of victims of war in the Middle East.

1903   Ameen Goryeb began publication of al-Mohajer (The Emi-
grant) a literary and informative weekly. The title
was significant for in it was the Arabic word hegira
meaning immigration and "mahjar" which had become New
York City, the Mecca of the New World. Kahlil Gibran
published his first work "al-Musiqa" in al-Mohajer.
Goryeb also encouraged Ameen Rihani and Abdul Massih
Haddad by publishing their writings.

Well-known in the business world of Washington, D.C.
is Mohammed Asa Abu-Howah, better known as A. Joseph
Howar. Howar's "Horatio Alger" story is a favorite
because of the oft-repeated dialogue which took place
upon his arrival in 1903 in New York as a Palestinian
immigrant lad of about seventeen. When asked by the
immigration officer as to where he was going, Howar,
not knowing, asked the officer "Where does your king
live?" He was informed that in America there was no
king, but rather a president who lived in Washington,
D.C. "Then I'll go to Washington, D.C. If it's good
enough for the president, then it's good enough for
me!" And so he went to Washington, D.C., and made
his fortune as a builder and became a moving spirit
as well as a financial backer of the building of the
Islamic Center there.

The first exhibition of paintings and wash drawings by
Kahlil Gibran was held at Wellesley College Wellesley,
Mass., on May 21st. In The Iris, Wellesley's Tau
Zeta Epsilon's annual publication, it was stated: Mr.
Gibran's work shows a wonderful originality in concep-
tion and an exquisite delicacy and fineness of execu-
tion."

Two Syrian brothers who manufactured gloves in Glovers-
ville, New York, sold $400,000 worth of their products
in this year.

1904   The St. Louis Exposition and World's Fair brought merchants and visitors from the Arab world. It also brought
back many performers who had originally come for the
Columbus Exposition and stayed on to settle in the
United States. It was also at the St. Louis Exposition
that the ice cream cone made its debut thanks to the
ingenuity of a Syrian wafflemaker. Apparently an ice
cream vendor ran out of plates and turned to his neigh-

bor , Ernest Hawmmi the wafflemaker in the next-door
booth. When he explained his predicament, Hawmi quickly twirled a waffle into the first cone which became
an overnight sensation as "World's Fair Cornucopias".

F. Holland Day, the well-known pictorial photograher,
held an exhibit of Khalil Gibran's drawings, studies,
and designs at Day's Studio in Boston. The show received major critical attention which greatly pleased
the twenty-one year old Mr. Gibran.
(See document No. 16)

1905   Arab-Americans of the Melkite Rite formally inaugurated
St. Joseph's Church in Lawrence, Massachussetts as the
first Melkite Parish Church in the United States. The
Church was blessed on Palm Sunday by Father James O'Reil-
ly, O.S.A., pastor of St. Mary's Church in Lawrence,
acting as Delegate of the Most Reverand John Joseph
Williams, Archbishop of Boston. The priest at St.
Joseph's parish was Father Philip Bata.
(See document No. 15)

1906   Farah Antoun moved the publication of his monthly magazine Aj-Jami'a (The League) from Cairo to New York
City. The magazine had advocated a secular state, a
mild form of socialism, religious freedom, tolerance
of western philosophies, and the independence of Egypt.
He thought he would find a more liberal atmosphere
among the Arab immigrants in America, but such was not
the case. After struggling for a number of years, Antoun returned to Egypt where he worked as a journalist
supporting Egyptian nationalists. His book, Ibn Rushd
(Averroes) and His Philosophy is considered one of the
best books to appear in the Arab world in the twentieth
century.

1907   A report to the United States Senate by the Immigration
Committee, after a visit to Turkey, stated that "the
Syrian immigrants send (home) more money per capita
than the immigrants of any other nationality. Between
Beirut and Damascus one sees numerous homes built with
American money, more than one would see in a trip five
times as long in Southern Italy."

1907   Al-Bakurat al-Durziyyah (The First Druse Organization)
was established by a group of young Druze men in Seat-
tle, Washington. Five branches were established in
Cleveland, Detroit, Butte, Akron, and Norfolk.

Immigration to the United States accelerated considerably when the Turkish government declared universal,
military conscription. Up to this time, Christians in
the Ottoman Empire had been able to avoid conscription
paying a fee.

The Syrian Union, an organization concerned with Syrian-American affairs, took up the South Carolina immigration case of a Syrian who had been denied citizenship by a certain Judge Smith who claimed Syrians were Asians and belonged to the yellow race, and were, therefore, ineligible for United States citizenship. The Syrian Union won the case, proving, as was necessary at that time, that Syrians belong to the Caucasian race.

1907   Nicholas Baida, art and rug dealer, built "The Castle". With its top floor observatory, it is considered one of Southern California's finest examples of Byzantine architecture.

The first Syrian-American Club was established in New York to strengthen the bonds between Syrian immigrants, to provide aid in the courts regarding immigration customs, to encourage naturalization, to protect their rights, and to in every way, enhance the Syrian name in their new home.

A survey by the Immigration Department indicated that of 9.188 Syrian immigrants admitted to the United States, 94% (8,725) declared they were coming to join relatives or friends.

1908   The first edition of the Syrian Business Directory was published jointly by S.A. Mokarzel, and H.F. Otash. It listed Arab-American business throughout the United States. Every state was included.

A Syrian in Toledo was building an aeroplane undaunted by the fact that his machine had been destroyed by storms three times.

The "Golden Link", an Arabic literary society was organized in Boston. Kahlil Gibran occasionally attended the meeting. The primary purpose of the organization was to discuss selections from the Arabic classics.

1909   A neighborhood in Chicago, near the railroad tracks was chosen by Syrian-Arab immigrants for housing because of the low rents. Their arrival in numbers killed off the saloon trade in the area (any liquor consumed was consumed only socially within the Syrian home) and drove off the disreputable inhabitants.

1910   The number of Arabic-speaking immigrants reached 6,317 in this year.

The Reports of the Immigration Commission for the 1899-1910 showed that the destinations named by the 56,909

Syrians admitted included every state in the Union,
and also Alaska, Hawaii, and Puerto Rico.

The first Chaldean Christians began arriving from Iraq.
They settled primarily in the Detroit area. By tradition the Chaldeans were "makari" or leaders of don-
key caravans from Iraq to Turkey. It is said that, in
the tradition of the old country, some of them walked
from Mexico to New York after arriving in the New World.

The Arabic-language newspaper Al-Bayan (The Statement)
was founded in New York City by Suleiman Baddour, a
Druze Moslem from the town of Ba'aklein, Lebanon. The
newspaper was originally dedicated to serve Druze affairs and news of the Druze Arab - American community.
Among its early editors and publishers were Ascad Mul-
ki, Ameen David, Massoud Sannaka and Said David. Raji
Daher became the editor and publisher in 1950. The
paper is known for having maintained a consistently
high literary and journalistic reputation.

As-Sayeh (The Traveler) a twice-weekly Arabic - language paper was founded by Nadra and Abdul Masseh Haddad, two Christian Orthodox brothers from Homs, Syria.
In 1921 it became the organ of the famous "Arrabitah"
(Association of the Pen), the literary Arab - American
group led by Khalil Gibran and including Abdul Masseh
Haddad. In 1957 Raji Daher bought As-Sayeh and consol-
idated it with Al-Bayan.

1911   It was estimated that in North Dakota there were about
800 Syrian farmers, and that there were 100 in the
neighborhood of Williston alone.

The Lebanon League of Progress was organized to express
the political aspirations of a large section of Lebanese
in the United States, Mexico and Canada.

The Arabic - language monthly Al-Funoon (The Arts) was
founded by Nassib Arida and Nazmi Nasseem, both Christian Orthodox from Homs, Syria. The magazine was popular. Nassib Arida was a recognized writer and poet, and
became a member of Gibran's "Arrabitah."

1912   Sumayeh Attujeh who had studied at the American Protestant Girl's School in Tripoli, Syria came to the United States to complete preparatory studies here and
then enter the field of medicine. She was subsequently asked to speak on the Near East, its history and
customs and spent the next fifteen years in the United States lecturing to American audiences.

Gibran's writings were attacked as sacreligious by Al-Mashriq, a Lenanese literary journal. By this year, he had published the following works in Arabic: Nubdah fi Fan al-Musiqa (Music) 1905; Ara'is al-Muruj (Nymphs of the Valley) 1906, Al-Arwah al-Mutamrridah (Spirits Rebellious) 1908, and Al-Ajnihah al-Mutakassirah (The Broken Wings).

THE MIDDLE PERIOD OF IMMIGRATION

1914 - 1945

Immigration dropped significantly during the period between World War I and World War II.

1914   Seventy families of Arabic-speaking origin were established in Utica, New York; forty of them operated grocery stores.

1915

"Ar-Rabitah" ("The Pen Bond" or Association of the Pen") was formed in New York City. Of all the literary societies and associations that appeared in the Arab world in the early twentieth century, "Ar-Rabitah Al-Kalamiyyah" which Khalil Gibran and his friends founded was the most outstanding. It had an enormous impact on Arabic literature, especially in its poetry. It brought forth new forms and styles which liberated Arabic poetry from ancient shackles. The poetry was unique in its lyrical style, form and freedom. Mikhail (Misha) Naimy's critical essays which were collected in a book called Al-Ghorbal (The Sieve) had tremendous impact on the literary Arab world. Members of "Ar-Rabitah al Kalamiyyah"" included Khalil Gibran, Mikhail Naimy, Elia Abu Madey, Nudra Hadda, Abdul Massih Haddad, Naseeb Arida, Ameen Rihani, William Catzeflis, Wadi Bahout, and Rashid Ayoub.

1916   The Maronite community (primarily Lebanese-Americans) under the leadership of N.A. Mokarzel, editor of Al-Hoda appealed to President Woodrow Wilson to intercede in the religious trouble of Mount Lebanon at this time.

Reverand Abraham Mitrie Ribhany's The Syrian Christ was published in book form by Houghton-Mifflin after chapters of it had appeared in the Atlantic Monthly. Rev. Ribhany's work was extremely well received as it offered an Oriental guide to Occidental readers of the Bible and provided a more intimate view of the Syrian environment in which the Scriptures were written.

April. The first Mass according to the Maronite rite
was said in the newly built St. Maron Church in Detroit,
Michigan. Joseph Shabaia, who had organized and built
several churches throughout the United States aided
the Detroit community in their venture. The first
appointed pastor of the church was Rev. Elias P. As-
mar who served the church until his death in 1933.
Rev. Peter S. Sfeir ministered to the parish until 1937
when he was succeeded by Rev. Michael Abdoo who remained pastor of the church until 1971.

1917   A number of Syrian and Lebanese Americans decided to
join the French Army which was about ot enter Syria.
The "League of Liberation" was also established in
New York. Its letterhead quoted President Wilson's
statement, "No people must be forced under soverignty
under which it does not wish to live." The League
encouraged young Syrian Americans to join the war
against Turkey. President of the League was Dr.
Ayub Tabet of New York.

In the Boston Evening Transcript of August 22nd, a
prominent social worker in the city is quoted as having said that in eight years of work in the Syrian
community of Boston, she had never seen a Syrian woman
intoxicated and had seen only one Syrian man in that
condition.

1918   Anis Fuleihan made his piano debut at Town Hall ren-
dering Bach and Liszt with "the subtlety and fervor
of an Oriental esthete as well as the skill and power
of an Occidental technician."

Based on United States government documents, 13,965
or about 7% of the Arab-American community served in
the United States Army during World War I.

1919   About 70,000 Arabic - speaking immigrants were supporting nine Arabic - language newpapers and magazines
and one English - languge magazine.

Rev. Abraham Mitrie Rihbany, Unitarian minister of the
Church of the Disciples in Brookline, Massachussetts
wrote America, Save the Near East. It was a thorough
presentation of the case of the Arab countries in the
post World War I era in English, by a person of the
Arab origin.

The Presbyterian Board of Foreign Missions reported
that as of December, it had transmitted $2,250,362
to Syrian relatives and friends from the Syrians in
America.

The American University of Beirut was opened in Beirut, Lebanon. A.U.B., as it has come to be known, has continued throughout the years as one of the strongest links of friendship between the United States and the Arab world.

1920   The Year Book of the Churches listed the Syrian Orthodox Church as having a membership of 50,000.

Lebanese-American painter Saliba Douweihy created the exquisite panels for Our Lady of Lebanon church in Brookly Heights, New York.

Mansour Farah started his clothing business in a 25 by 500 foot building near the union depot in El Paso, Texas. His sons, William and James, built Farah into a $165 million slacks empire.

1923   The Prophet by Khalil Gibran was published by Alfred Knopf. It became one of the all-time best selling books in America. Within one month the first edition of 1300 copies was sold.
                        (See document No. 19)

1924   United States Senate immigration legislation decreed that 925 Syrians, or three percent of those who were born in Syria and who were in the United States in 1910, could be admitted per year into the United States. This quota was to be distributed over five months beginning in July and ending in November. It also stated that special preference was to be given to applicants who had immediate relatives who were naturalized citizens of the United States.

Dr. Philip K. Hitti, Princeton scholar, wrote The Syrians in America, which was published by Doran and Company.

1925   A group of Moslem immigrnats in Cedar Rapids, Iowa, who rented a building to serve as a mosque, formed an organization to bind themselves together religiously, socially, and culturally. This was known as "The Rose of Fraternity Lodge." These Syrian peddlars, as they were known, looked forward to the day when a real mosque would grace their community.

In support of the uprising in Syria to gain independence from the French, the Syrian Federation was formed. It had the effect of awakening some political consciousness in the Arab - American immigrant communities and

raised some large sums of money for the cause. The
Maronite Christian Arab - American community, under
the leadership of Al-Hoda's publisher, Naoum Mokarzel,
continued to call for a Christian state in Lebanon under French protection.
                    (See document No. 20)

1926   The Arabic Monthly Al Khalidat was established by Rev.
            Anthony Bashir. This young clergyman became particu-
            larly adept in the difficult task of translating from
            English into Arabic. In this role, he opened up an
            entire new world to the Arab literary mind, translating
            such works as: Crane's, Why I am a Christian, Tolstoy's
            Confessions, Wagner's Simple Life and many others. Al-
            though Arabic was the mother tongue of the great Leba-
            nese poet, Khalil Gibran, he chose to entrust Archi-
            mandrite Bashir with the Arabic translation of his ma-
            jor works: The Prophet, Sand and Foam, The Madman,
            and The Earth of Gods. When he saw the results, Gibran
            wrote to the Archimandriet, "Only you could have tail-
            ored such a beautiful Arabic garment for my Prophet."

            Publication of The Syrian World, an English - language
            monthly magazine began to provide a link to the old
            country and to those second generation Arab - Americans
            who were not fluent in the Arabic language. The aim
            of the publication was to serve as a forum for the dis-
            cussion of the existing problems of the Syrians in
            America, to present conditions and affairs in Syria,
            and to chronicle Syrian achievements in the arts and
            business.
                    (See document No. 21)

1927   A conference of the Greater New York Arabic writers,
            business and professional men was held. They saw their
            task to be one of education, to dispel inferiority
            feelings among the immigrant community and to better
            interpret themselves to the American communities.

            Elia D. Mady published his renowned volume of poetry
            Al-Jadawil. He had emigrated from Lebanon to the Uni-
            ted States in 1911. In 1920 when "Al-Rabitah" (The
            Pen League) was born, Madey joined Gibran, Rihani and
            the others in this renaissance of Arabic poetry. With
            the publicaiton of Al-Jadawil, Madey, or Abu Madey as
            he was known, became well-known throughout the Arab-
            American community. In 1929, Madey started As-Sameer
            which became a well-recognized Arabic language maga-
            zine throughout America. Madey's fourth volume of
            poetry, Al-Khama'il, was published in 1940 and his
            fifth volume, Tibr wa-Turab, was published after his
            death in 1957.

1928   Other Arabian Nights by H.I. Katibah was published by
            Charles Scribners' Sons. As the book reviewer, Nagla
            M. Lafloofy, M.D., said, "Other Arabian Nights is a
            delightful collection of Arabic folk lore. It is
            somehow strange to see these familiar tales in a western
            setting, written in English and beautifully illustrated
            by William Berger, already famous in America for his
            technique. In spite of the western clothing, Mr. Katibah
            manages to retain the Middle Eastern flavor of these
            stories. There are nineteen of them."

            Toofik Simon managed and directed the Arabia Troupe
            which the press called "one of the most colorful groups
            at the Pacific Southwest Exposition."

1929   Ameen Rihani and M.W. Weisgal debated the question of
            the "Rights in Palestine of Jews." The discussion
            was carried in the New York Times of October 27th.

            As-Sameer (The Entertainer) was founded in New York City
            in 1929 as a magazine by Elia Abu Madey, an orthodox
            Christian from El-Muhaydithah, Lebanon. As Sameer en-
            joyed little financial success and Madey had a very hard
            time making a living from it. When his father-in-law,
            Mr. Diab of Al-Meraat, died in 1935 he moved As Sameer
            to Brooklyn and published it as a daily five times a week;
            After World War II it was published three times a week.
            He continued to publish it until his death in 1957.
            He was his own editor, assisted by Fred G. Koury, who
            after Madey's death, became associated with Al-Hoda.

            Habib Katibah was the special correspondent in the Near
            East for the Brooklyn Daily Eagle, The Boston Globe
            and Detroit News. Mr. Katibah wrote on the experiences
            of Arab - Americans returning to visit the "Old Countries"
            as well as on activities of the Arab immigrants in Amer-
            ican communities.
                (See documents No. 18 and No. 22)

            Louis J. Hazan wrote The Pig With the Straight Tale for
            children aged ten through twelve.

            Professor Philip Hitti state that "a census taken in
            1929 lists 102 Arabic periodicals and papers which saw
            the light in the U.S.A."

            The San Francisco Zoological Gardens, formerly known
            as the "Fleishhacker Zoo" was first organized by George
            Maroon Bistany. Bistany, a wild animal collector,
            was induced to come to San Francisco to start the Zoo
            by Mr. Herbert Fleishhacker, a philanthropist who was
            President of the San Fransisco Park Commission. After
            Mr. Bistany's untimely death in 1935, Mr. John Mallick,

also an Arab - American, served in various super-
visory positions for thirty-seven years. The Zoo is
one of the main attractions and pride of the City of
San Francisco.

A testimonial dinner was given in honor of Mr. Ameen
Rihani, who was a prolific writer in both English and
Arabic. Among his outstanding accomplishments are:
"The Book of Khaled", a satire on a young Syrian immigrant in New York, his translation of The Luzumiyat by the
Arabic poet-philosopher Abu'l-Ala, his own poetry,
including A Chart of Mystics and Other Poems, and his
writings on Ibn-al-Saoud and the Najd which in the words
of Philip Hitti "pushed the wall a little back between
the known and the unknown."

About Rihani's Maker of Modern Arabia, the New York
Times said, "From Ameen Rihani we have what can scarce-
ly fail to be a final portrait of that formidable
Chieftan, Ibn Sa'oud, by right of conquest, King of
Mecca."

Fred Saideh, scenario writer in Hollywood and contri-
butor to the "Conning Tower" column of the New York
Herald Tribune co-authored the musical-comedy hit,
"Bloomer Girl."

Khalil Gibran was the recipient of a testimonial dinner
at the Hotel Mc Alphin in New York City, honoring his
twenty-five years of contribution to Arabic letters.
            (See document No. 23)

1930   July. At Symphony Hall the Boston Syrian Tercentenary
Committee presented a celebration of historical and
cultural aspects of Syrian -Arabs in the United States.

A Syrian-American Club was formed in Tucson, Arizona.
This club represented a new trend of thought among the
young and was non-sectarian. Its objectives included
better understanding between Syrians and Americans as
well as social and political activities.

Syrians of the Boston area joined other ethnic groups
in a protest against the lowering of immigrant quotas
by the United States government.

            (See document No. 26)

The "mahrajan" or outdoor picnic was inaugurated on
August 31, in Bridgeport, Connecticut, and soon was
copied by other Arab - American communities throughout
the United States.
            (See document No. 25)

1930   Arab-American writer Ameen Rihani authored the book, <u>Around the Coast of Arabia</u>, had three articles published in <u>Travel</u> magazine, and was covered by the <u>New York Times</u> when he spoke out on his political ideas in an article entitiled: "Sees Zionist Aims Imperiling Peace; Syrian Poet Declars Balfour Declaration Must be Revoked to Avert Uprising," on January 19, 1930.

The Syrian American Directory Almanac was published in New York City. It covered New York City and Brooklyn and included a "Business Directory" and "Residence Directory" for each borough. There were 232 pages in English and 283 pages in Arabic. In the <u>Classified Business Directory</u>, two interesting advertisements appear:

    ARTISTS
      Gibran, Kahlil
        51 W. 10th. St.   ALGonquin 9709

    LAWYERS
      Ferris, Miss Emeline
        291 Broadway   WORth 6212

In the "Organizational Listings" section is found the "Syrian Hebrew Aid Society" tucked in its place between the "Syrian Ladies Aid Society" and the "Syrian Merchants Association, Grocery Division." The book is a microcosm of the Arab-American immigrant community in the United States, listing everything from importing companies to furnished rooms, professional offices, where to get piano lessons and the availability of Syrian pastries.

1931   After the death of Naoum Mokarzel, his brother, Salloum, succeeded him as publisher of <u>Al-Hoda</u>. Salloum Mokarzel had previously published the English-language monthly, <u>The Syrian World</u>. He became as powerful a leader as his brother had been among the Maronite Arab-Americans. He consistently championed Lebanese causes.

Dr. Michael A. Shadid established the first cooperative hospital, the Community Hospital of Elk City in Western Oklahoma. Dr. Shadid told the story of the founding of the hospital in his book <u>Crusading Doctor</u>.

Reverend Abraham Mitri Rihbany began his ministry of the Unitarian church in Boston, Massachussetts. He served this American congregation with much distinction for many years. During this period he authored his well-known <u>The Syrian Christ</u> and wrote articles for the <u>Antlantic Monthly.</u>

The Southern Federation of Syrian Lebanes American
Clubs was founded in 1931. The first convention was
held in 1932, and H.S. Amuny became the organization's
first president. Within ten years, the Federation
had expanded to the East Coast. They have published
"The Official Bulletin" since 1936, which is now edited
by Kamal Antone. Its activities have included relief
of the Middle Eastern conflicts and to natural disaster
victims in Syria, Lebanon and, also, in America. Scholarship funds have been given in the amount of over
$100,000. Donations are made to the Center for Middle
Eastern Studies at the University of Texas in Austin.
The organization is comprised of about seventy clubs
in over fifty southern cities and has a total membership exceeding 2.700. It provides a forum in which
Arabic-speaking people can foster their customs, music,
language, folklore, hospitality, and devotion to heritage. It is a non-political, non-sectarian organization.

1932   Sam Mamey founded and published the Syrian American
            News. This was the first newspaper on the West Coast
            for the American-Arabic community.

            Towfiek Malouf of the Syrian - American Club of Boston
            called together representatives of Syrian - American
            Clubs from Quincy, Lawrence, Worcester, Massachussetts,
            Pawtucket and Central Falls, Rhode Island, and New Lon-
            don, Connecticut. The "Syrian American Federation of
            New England" was thus established. This federation
            later became known as the Eastern States Federation.

1933   Al Islaah (The Reform) began publication. Fawzi Braidy,
            a Melkite Lebanese from Zahle was the first editor.
            In 1950, Dr. Alphonze Chaurize, a Chaldean priest,
            took over ownership of Al-Islaah. He has published it
            since then without religious orientation. The paper
            has a steady circulation of one thousand readers through-
            out the world. The masthead reads, "Serving the People
            with the Light of the Truth."

1934   The "Syrian American Federation of New England" changed
            its name to the "Syrian and Lebanese American Federation
            of the Eastern States."
            (See document No. 33)

            Elias Shamoon was the first Arab - American to be
            appointed to a judgeship. Judge Shamoon was appointed
            by Governor Saltonstall of Massachusetts.

            The first place of worship in North America specifically
            designed and built as a mosque was completed in Cedar
            Rapids, Iowa. It has been referred to as the "Mother

Mosque" in North America. Two highly respected imams
who led the congregation during the early days in Ce-
dar Rapids were Kamil Al-Hind from Damascus and Shaykh
Khalil Al-Rawof from the Njad (northern Saudi Arabia).
The families immediately set up a progran for prayer,
Arabic lessons and social affairs.
                     (See document No. 28)

May 25. Dr. Rosa Lee Neimer, a graduate of Johns Hopkins University, gave a scholarly paper on the serum
treatment of pneumonia in children. Dr. Neimer was
an instructor in the New York Medical School and Belle-
vue College in pediatrics and a research fellow in
pneumonia.

June 17. Arab - Americans of the East Coast came together for the first Syrian World Athletic Meet held
in Atlantic Highlands, New Jersey.

The Syrian Fine Arts Guild was organized by Alice Mokarzel and Mrs. Joseph Ferris. The highlight of the
year was a concert given at the Swendenborg Church
in Brooklyn. This concert gathered together the Syrian-
Lebanese artists in the greater New York area, such as
Litia Namoura of the Ruth St. Dennis Dance Co.; Helen
Rosek Walker, violinist with the Women's Symphony;
Selma Boujalad, singer with the "Hansel and Gretel"
opera; and Elvira Helal who later sang leading operatic
roles with the Chicago Civic Opera.

1935   Selma Bojalad of Cleveland, Ohio sang the title role
              of Hansel in a command performance at the White House.
              Miss Bojalad was a member of the National Music League's
              group of young artists.

              Esa Halow became an artist noted for his originality
              and rare sense of color. "There is a quality in his
              work that reflects an individuality of genuine and
              poetic charm. The Orient, America, and the war encour-
              aged and abetted his artistic ambitions."

              John Gannam became an outstanding illustrator in Col-
              liers, Good Housekeeping, and The Ladies Home Journal.

1936   The Arab League in America was born under the leader-
              ship of Dr. Foud Shatara, a Palestinian from the town
              of Ramallah and Habib I. Katibah from Mabk, Syria.
              Its main purpose was to fight Zionism in America and
              to help Palestian Arabs in their struggle both against
              the British and Zionists. It was a fairly successful
              venture, sepecially among the Palestinian immigrants.

              Wadie Rashid Khouri's poetry collection, Neda' a Al-Ghab

was published with an introduction by Elia Abu Mady.
Khouri is an authority on Arabic literature in "al-
Mahjar" (the Americas).

The Midwest Federation of American Syrian-Lebanese
Clubs was founded. Its original name was the Midwest
Federation of American Syrian Clubs. The Federation
holds an annual convention in August. The first president of the organization was Dr. Waheeb S. Zarick of
Indianapolis, Indiana. In 1940 a scholarship program
was initiated which is still active today. In fact,
Michael J. Coury, 1977 President of the Midwest Federation, was a former winner of the Federation scholarship.

Reverend Anthony Bashir was named Archbishop of the
North American Antiochian Church at St. Nicholas Cathedral in Brooklyn, New York in the presence of thousands
of delegates from the entire Western Hemisphere. Samuel David was named Archbishop of Toledo and its envi-
rons at impressive cermonies.

1937   "Zionism Decried by Arab Leader; Expansion Must be
Stopped to End Strife in Palestine, Ameen Rihani says
here." This headline was carried above an article in
the New York Times on June 16th., as Ameem Rihani,
Habib Katibah and other politically aware Arab-Americans
tried to bring what was happening in Palestine to the
attention of the American people.

February. Metropolitan Anthony Bashir became the first
Archbishop of the Antiochian Orthodox Church to open
a session of the U.S. House of Representatives with a
paryer.

Professor Philip Hitti of Princeton University published
his History of the Arabs (by Macmillan). The 767 page
book was a "Scholarly and authoritative history, -an
opus magnus" according to the New York Times book re-
viewer.

1938   Harvard University honored the one-thousand-year anniversary of the birth of Abu'l Ula Al Muarri, the great
philosopher-poet of the Arab world. Ameen Rihani translated The Quatrains of Abu'l Ula from Arabic to English
in 1903. Rihani is quoted as saying, "I am proud to
be of that nation which had that liberal brave poet."

1139   Habib I. Katibah's New Spirit In Arab Lands was pub-
lished. Mr. Katibah, a graduate of the Harvard Divinity
School, joined other distinguished Arab-Americans, Dr.
Ameen Faris, Dr. Ismail El Khalidi, and Dr. Khalil Totah,
at the Office of War Information and later organized the
Institute of Arab-American Affairs.

Salom Rizk who came to the United States as an immigrant in his late teens was commissioned by the Readers,
Digest to tell his story to high school audiences throughout the United States. (This story was published by
Doubleday in 1952 under the title, Syrian Yankee).

1940   James Ansara became Executive Secretary of the Nation-
            al Federation of American Syrian Lebanese Clubs and
            the Federation Herald became the official publication
            of the organization.

1944   Clifford Saber, famed for his repertorial watercolor
            paintings of World War II, executed a series of murals
            at Rockefeller Center. Mr. Saber is said to be the
            first artist in the United States to apply linoleum
            in painting.

                  THE PERIOD OF THE LATER IMMIGRATION
                           1945 - 1977

This period has witnessed the arrival of more than
100,000 Arabs to the United States shores. These new
arrivals differed from their predecessors in that many
more came from Iraq, Egypt, Yemen, Palestine, Morocco,
and other countries of the Arab world as well as Syria
and Lebanon. Also, while the early immigrants had
been predominantly Christians, 70% of theses newcomers
were Moslem and were educated in the United States and
Europe.

1945   The Arab - American Institute was organized in New
            York City under the leadership of Habib I. Katibah, Dr.
            Khalil Totah, Ismail Khalidi and Joseph Sado. For the
            four years it was active, its concern was the political
            events which were taking place in the Middle East, par-
            ticularly the beginnings of trouble in Palestine.

1946   December 10. This day marked the fifteenth anniver-
            sary of Kahlil Gibran's death. He was eulogized by
            A.J. Philpott in Boston, the city of his youth.
                  (See document No. 32)

            Echo of the East, an Arabic English Monthly Magazine
            was published in Detroit, Michigan.

            The Western Federation of Americans of Arabic Heritage
            was formed in San Francisco by three or four clubs
            from San Francisco and Los Angeles. Later it expanded
            to cover organizations in Seattle, Portland, Phoenix,
            San Diego, Oakland, Las Vegas. The annual Conventions
            are held in various cities with the local organizations
            acting as the host club.

Dr. Michael A. Shadid was elected first president of
the newly established Cooperative Health Federation of
America.

1947   The Hosn Welfare Association was founded in New Kensing-
ton, Pennsylvania, for the purpose of helping their
town of El-Hosn in Syria. It was decided that the Association would build a hospital in that town, which
they did after raising over half a million dollars.
The Association still continues to make up the hospital's annual deficit.

1948   The outbreak of war in Palestine awakened the nation-
alistic sentiments of the Arab - American communities.

The Palestine Dilemma was written by Frank Sakran, an
Arab - American who was Chief Legal Consultant to the
Board of Veterans Appeals.

The first independently-owned and desiganted Moslem
cemetary in North America was created in Cedar Rapids,
Iowa, when Hajj William Yahya Aossey set aside six and
one-half acres of land that was to be owned by the
Moslem community and was to be used for all Moslems
everywhere.

The first Chaldean Catholic parish was founded in Detroit where eighty Arab - American families had already
settled. These families were all from Iraq, 96% came
from the city of Telkeppe (Telkaif), the other 4% from
surrounding villages in northern Iraq. There are five
Chaldean parishes in the United States and the liturgy
and masses are spoken in Syro-Chaldaic or Aramaic,
which is recognized to have been the language spoken
by Jesus Christ. Reverend Thomas Bidawid was the first
pastor of the Mother of God Church. By 1973 membership
had grown to such an extent that there was a need for
a second parish. This church was called the Sacred
Heart. Reverend Jacob Yasso was assigned to the Sacred
Heart Parish. The Right Reverend Monsignor George
Garmo ministers to the Mother of God Parish. The two
parishes together claim a membership of more than
8,000.

George A. Hamid received the Horatio Alger award from
the American Schools and Colleges Association in New
York. Hamid who concurrently owned Atlantic City's
famed Steel Pier and the Million Dollar Pier began
his career as a tumbler in the streets of his Lebanese
village.
                (See document No. 44)

The Syrian - Lebanese Federation inaugurated the policy of giving honorary awards to men and women of Arabic-speaking origin in the United States who excel in any field of human endeavor. The 1948 award went to Dr. Michael Shadid, the eminent physician in cooperative hospitalization.

1949
The Islamic Center in Washington, D.C. was completed. The Center is an artistic monument to Islamic culture. It was built with funds from American citizens as well as funds from Islamic countries around the world. Both the mosque for worship and the Institute for the higher study of the Islamic culture are open to visitors. Dr. Abdul Rauf was appointed imam of the Center in the early 1960's.

Dr. Majid Khadduri, Iraqi-born authority on Islamic law, became professor at the Johns Hokins University School of Advanced International Studies. Dr. Khadduri received his Ph.D. from the University of Chicago, was a member of Iraq's delegation to the founding of the United Nations in San Francisco and is a widely-read author in his field. His classic work is The Law of War and Peace in Islam.

The Syrian - Lebanese Federation award to an outstanding Arab - American went to Dr. Philip K. Hitti, the renowned scholar and historian of the Arabs.

1950
The outstanding Arab - American award was presented to George Hamid, the noted impressario.

The first in a series of international conventions took Arab - Americans back to Syria and Lebanon for what was called "The Convention of the Absent Ones" or "The Overseas Convention." The convention which was one month in length (two weeks in Syria and two weeks in Lebanon) was organized by the Syrian -Lebanese Federation of the Eastern states in conjunction with the other federations now known as the National Association of Syrian - Lebanese Federations. The presiding officer of the convention was Frank Maria and the convention chairmam was Joseph Sado. A number of meetings took place between the Coordinating Committee of the National Association of Syrian - Lebanese Federations and members of the United States Department of State prior to the Overseas Convention. The Department of State looked upon the convention as an opportunity to further better relations between the United States and the Arab world. It was known in Dr. Maria's words as a "people to people" program.
(See document No. 41)

The "National Association of Federations of Syrian and
Lebanese American Clubs" was formed. This included
the memberships of the Eastern, Southern and Midwestern
Federations. The National Herald became the publication of the organization and James Batal was editor.

The Hamra-Homra Family Club was organized in the Tri-
States area of Southeast Missouri, Northwest Tennesee,
and Southwest Kentucky. The purpose of the club was
to keep those Arab-Americans from Judeidet Merjayoun
in touch with their hometown and their heritage.

Assignment: Near East by James Batal was published
by Friendship Press. Mr. Batal is also the co-author
of Most of the World and Your Newspaper. Born in Lawrence, Massachusetts, Mr. Batal served with the Office
of War information in Cairo and while lecturing in
journalism at the American University of Beirut also
served as faculty advisor for student publications.

1951   October 2. A delegation of seven representatives who
            had attended the Overseas Convention of the Syrian
            Lebanese Federation met with President Harry Truman
            at the White House. The two main purposes of the meet-
            ing were:
                1.   President Truman wanted to thank the National
                     Association of Syrian - Lebanese Federations
                     for the results of the Convention.
                2.   The Federations wished to share their recommen-
                     dations on United States policy toward the
                     Middle East.

            Arab - Americans and other concerned Americans met with
            columnist Dorothy Thompson to found the American Friends
            of the Middle East (A.F.M.E.). The goal of A.F.M.E. was
            stated as a "desire to promote common spiritual bonds
            between the United States and the Arabic - speaking
            countries." Prominent in this meeting were Dean Vir-
            ginia Gildersleeve, Rev. Harry Emerson Fosdick of the
            Baptist Church, and Princeton scholar, Dr. Philip K.
            Hitti.

            Danny Thomas, comedian and entertainer was awarded
            the honor of outstanding American of Arabic - speaking
            origin by the American Syrian - Lebanese Federation
            in its annual awards ceremony.

1952   The Federation of Islamic Associations in the United
            States and Canada was created. (It was originally
            called "The International Muslim Society"). The idea
            for this organization took root during world War II
            when Abdallah Igram, a second - generation Arab - Ameri-
            can who was serving as an officer in the United States

Armed Forces, realized how great the lack of information regarding Islam was among Americans. He was particularly concerned that the Moslem soldier should be given an "X" indentification.

(See documents No. 34 and No. 35)

Mary Mokarzel took over publication of Al Hoda after the death of her father, Salloum Mokarzel.

Hathihe Ramallah magazine began publication. This magazine serves those people who immigrated from the city of Ramallah, located about ten miles north of Jerusalem.

Syrian Yankee, Salom Rizk's autobiography was published by Doubleday. The book was an amplification of the authobiographical story which Rizk told for years on the lecture circuit and which describes the unlimited opportunities, freedom, and fullness of life which he found available in the United States.

Major James Jabara, the first American jet-pilot ace received the award as outstanding American of Arabic - speaking background from the Federation of American Syrian Lebanese Clubs.

June 27-29. The first International Muslim Convention for the United States and Canada was held in Cedar Rapids, Iowa. The Muslim Star became the news organ of the Federation.

1953   James Ansara was hired as the full-time executive officer of the National Association of Federations of Syrians and Lebanese American Clubs, and offices were set up in Washington, D.C. President Eisenhower sent greetings to the organization on this occasion
(See document No. 36)

Najeeb Halaby won the United States Chamber of Commerce's Arthur Fleming Award as the "outstanding young man in Federal Service." In 1948 Mr. Halaby became Foreign Affairs Advisor to Secretary of Defense James Forrestal under President Harry Truman. He helped organize the North Atlantic Treaty Organization (NATO) and completed his Pentagon career as Deputy Assistant Secretary of Defense for Internatinal Security Affairs in 1954 under President Dwight D. Eisenhower. In 1961 Mr. Halaby was appointed to the top civil aviation job, Federal Aviation Agency Administrator.

1954   B.D. Eddie of Oklahoma City was elected to the Board of Trustees of the American University of Beirut.

Eddie has been credited with perhaps contributing
more to the growth and development of the feed manufacturing industry than any other man in the Southwestern United States according to national industry
leaders.

February 23. Rosalind Elias made her debut at the
Metropolitan Opera House as Grimgerde in Richard Wagner's
"Die Walduere." Elias, a native of Lowell, Massachusetts, won the Met contract as a result of competing
in the Metropolitan Opera Auditions of the Air.

1955   A beautiful mosque was erected in Toledo, Ohio. A
number of second-generation Moslems from other parts
of the United States moved to Toledo because of the
mosque. The Toledo Moslem community exemplified to
them an active and articulate Moslem group in the
United States.
    (See documents No. 37 and No. 38)

1956   Crusading Doctor was published by Meador Publishing
Co. in Boston. This book is the autobiographical
account of Michael Shadid's boyhood in Lebanon, his
immigration to the United States at age sixteen, his
pursuit of a medical education and his years as a
physician in Missouri and Oklahoma. The "Crusade"
was his twenty-year struggle to implement his belief
in the principle of cooperative medicine.

Fe Al Mahajer el Amerekkeya (Our Cultural Leaders in
the Americas) was written by George Seydah in Arabic
and translated into English by Michael Cahaly of Boston.

1957   The Syrian Antiochian Orthodox Archdiocese began publication of The Word in English. This official journal
of the church had been known by its Arabic title,
Al Kalimat, since its publication began in January,
1905.

W.N. (Nick) Kerbawy, general manager of the Detroit
Lions, led his team to its third National Football
League championship.

1958   At the October Convention of the American Public Health
Association in St. Louis, Missouri, Dr. Abdel Rabim
Omran, graduate of Cairo University, doing graduate
work at Columbia University, presented a paper which
revealed new hope for thousands of unknown TB victims
living in the vast underdeveloped areas of the world.
Dr. Omran's theory provided skin tests for all Nava-
jo youngsters under twelve years of age. The families
of those showing positive reactions were then examined

by the traditional x-rays, sputum examination and
lab tests. This way, the necessity for testing the
whole community was avoided.

1959   March 12. The start of the Moslem month of Ramadan,
              a 30-day period of fasting was announced on page one
              of the Toledo Blade.
                        (See document No. 39)

              Seven mosques in the United States received complete
              libraries from the United Arab Republic. Eighty per
              cent of the books were in English and twenty per cent
              in Arabic.
                        (See document No. 40)

              Michael J. Damas was elected mayor of Cleveland, Ohio.
              One of the most significant contributions of his ad-
              ministration was the establishment of the Medical
              College of Ohio at Toledo.

              The American Ramallah Federation was founded in Detroit,
              Michigan as a result of the first Convention called by
              Hathihe Ramallah Magazine. Since then 16 Annual Conven-
              tions have been held in almost every major city of
              the United States where a large Ramallah community
              resides. The Federation is composed of about fifteen
              Ramallah local clubs representing almost every Ramallah
              community in the United States. Its objectives are
              social, educational, charitable, and cultural. It
              also promotes understanding and goodwill between Arabs
              and Americans hoping to contribute to better understand-
              ing of the Palestinian problem. The major accomplish-
              ment of the Federation has been in aid given to needy
              families in Ramallah and the West Bank of Jordan, and
              by providing assistance and encouragement through an
              Educational and Scholarship Fund.

1960   AMARA (American Arabic Association) was started in
              Boston. The Boston chapter has been one of its most
              active in humanitarian activities. It conducts an an-
              nual fund-raising campaign in support of the Musa Ala-
              mi project in Jericho, which houses and trains home-
              less refugee orphan boys. AMARA has also taken a
              leading role in finding sponsors of Palestinian child-
              ren for Project Ryaiat; more than 65 Ryaiat children
              are now being helped through AMARA.

              The American Druze Society of the Greater Los Angeles
              Area was formally established. It is a part of the
              much older national organization, also known as the
              ADS, which is located in the State of Michigan. The
              membership in the Greater Los Angeles Area consists
              mostly of Arabs of the Druze faith, although many

active members are Americans or Arabs of other faiths
The purpose of the ADS is to foster and organize social
and cultural activies amongst the membership.
    (See document No. 43)

Metropolitan Anthony Basheer was the first bishop of the
Antiochian Orthodox Church to join the National Council
of Churches.

During the 1960's large numbers of Yemeni, Palestinian,
Lebanese and Iraqis were employed in Detroit's auto in-
dustry. Of the approximately 85,000 Arabs living in
Michigan, nearly 15,000 are auto workers.

1960   St. Jude Hospital was established in Memphis, Tennessee, dedicated by Danny Thomas and the Association
of Lebanese - Syrian - American Clubs (ALSAC).
    (See document No. 42)

George Coury was the first Arab-American to buy a
seat on the New York Stock Exchange.

Kareem T. Salem of Akron, Ohio was awarded the "Knight
of the Cedar" medal by the Lebanese government in recognition of his humanitarian service.

1961   Dr. Aziz S. Atiya founded the Middle East Studies Center at the University of Utah, Salt Lake City.

A Group of women in the San Francisco Bay area organized the NAJDA (Women Concerned About the Middle East).
This organization has been most active in bringing
together Arab-American women to study the Middle East
and raise money for UNRWA (United Nations Relief and
Work Agency) Palestinian student scholarships. This
organization also prublishes a monthly newsletter sur-
veying all activities of interest to those in the
San Francisco Bay area concerned with Middle East and
Arab-American affairs. The newsletter has a wide circulation throughout the United States, for it also
digests and reprints articles from other major publications. Najda has printed an Arabic Cookbook and
members Ruth Afife, Jean Pelletiere and Audrey Shabbas
have worked with Professor Ayad Al-Qazzaz of California State University, Sacramento, in his survey of
The Arabs in American Textbooks. The first president
of the organization was Mrs. Pat Daoud.

US OMEN (United States Organization for Medical and
Educational Needs) was founded by Arab-Americans in
California to provide assistance in the fields of
medical-dental aid and education, wherever the need

is most acute. US Omen works through organizations
such as UNRWA, CARE, and other recognized groups carrying on humanitarian work throughout the world. It is
a non-profit organizatization chartered under the laws of
the State of California. OMEN has generated $280,000
assistance in cash to Palestinian refugees and other
victims in the Middle East in addition to pharmaceuticals
and medical equipment worth more than one million dollars. It has established refugee scholarship loans at
several Middle East universities and assisted orphanages
and schools helping refugee children.

Dr. Frank Maria of Warner, New Hampshire, was cited by
President Eisenhower for a "contribution of outstanding
and unprecedented value" when he served as the first
Arab - American on the United States delegation to
UNESCO.

1962   Dr. Philip K. Hitti's Islam: A Way of Life was pub-
            lished by the University of Minnesota Press. In
            his book review Rabbi Nahum Schulman, professor of the
            Jay Philips Chair of Jewish Studies at St. John's Uni-
            versity, Collegeville, Minnesota, said, "It is lucid,
            scholarly, objective, readable, and offers a timely
            contribution to the field of historical religions and
            their impact upon civilization."

1964   The Action Committee on American-Arab Relations was
            created as a reaction to Zionist efforts at the New
            York World's Fair to prevent the Jordan Pavillion from
            displaying a mural which was a poem about the Palestinian
            refugees. The American Jewish Congress and the Anti-
            Defamtion League began picketing the Jordanian Pavillion
            and Dr. M.T. Mehdi requested permission from Robert
            Moses, President of the Fair, for a group of Arab-
            Americans to picket the Isreali Pavillion. This was
            the beginning of the Action Committee on American-Arab
            Relations.

            George Kasem was the first Arab-American to enter the
            United States House of Representarives. Victor Atiyeh
            served as Oregon State Senator.

            The Islamic Center of New England was dedicated in
            Quincy, Massachusetts. Sam Hassan, whose father and
            uncles had immigrated to the Quincy area in 1902, became
            the first president of the center.

1965   Prior to 1965 immigration to the United States from
            the "Asia-Pacific Triangle", which includes the Arab
            countries, was limited to two thousand persons per
            year, excluding relatives and kin. The change in the
            law in 1965 opended immigratin to the educated and

and those having talents needed by the United States.
Approximately 37,600 Arabs in professional and related
occupations immigrated to the United States during the
period 1968 - 1970.

The American Arab Society, a non-profit organization,
was formed for the purpose of providing those individuals of Palestinian descent, and also those who have
affinity with them, and who permanently reside in the
California area, with a social and charitable organization. The original name chosen was The American
Jordanian-Palestinian Society. In 1973 the name was
changed to the American-Arab Society. It publishes
"Unity", a monthly newsletter.

Ralph Nader wrote Unsafe at Any Speed, "The Designed-
in Dangers of the American Automobile." The book was
published by Grossman and created a stinging attack on
Nader by General Motors. Having weathered the attack
this proved to be the beginning of Nader's role as consumer advocate extraordinaire.

John V. Lindsay, the mayor of New York City, failed to
offer the common courtesy of receiving King Feisal of
Saudi Arabia who was a guest of the President of the
United States and the American Government. This was
in sharp contrast to the welcome provided to Ahamd Bin
Na'aman on his visit to New York City in 1840.

1966   Archimandrite Philip Saliba, pastor of St. George's
            Church, Cleveland, Ohio, was elected Archbishop for
            the Archdiocese of New York and all North America.

The Exarchate of the Maronite Rite of the Roman Catholic Church in the United States was established in
Detroit, Michigan. In June, 1972, the Exarchate was
raised to the full rank of Diocese by Pope Paul, and
Bishop Francis Zayek received his staff as first Bishop of the new Maronite Diocese in America. The new
diocese included 150,000 people in forty-three parishes.

A "Medresa" (Weekend Islamic School) for children of
Arab - American families was established in Rockville,
Maryland under the leadership of Dr. A.S. Hashim.

Farhat J. Ziadeh joined the faculty of Near East Studies
at the University of Washington. Dr. Ziadeh has written a history of the American people for the Arabs.

Abraham Kazen, Jr. was elected to the United States
House of Representatives from Texas. In 1952, he was
elected to the Texas State Senate after serving in the

Texas House of Representatives. The son of a Lebanese
immigrant, Kazen's legislative activity in Texas cen-
tered on education. In addition, he was the author of
bills creating pre-school programs for non-English
speaking children. In the United States House of Representatives, Mr. Kazen served on the Foreign Affairs Committee and the Committee on Interior and Insular Affairs.

James R. Deeb was elected to the Florida State Senate.
He formerly served in the Florida House and is now
serving as minority party leader pre tempore in the
Senate. The senator has also participated actively in
the activities of the Southern Federation of Syrian
Lebanese Clubs.

1967   As a result of the outbreak of hostilities between Israel and the Arab states in June, the hierarchy of the
American Near Eastern Christian Church- Orthodox, Melkite, Maronite and Armenian - met in Boston and formed
the Near East Bishops Emergency Relief Fund. A joint
letter of appeal was sent to President Johnson. Bishop Philip Saliba, of the Orthodox Church, met with President Johnson to express his concern regarding the
plight of the Palestinian refugees.

The Association of Arab-American University Graduates
(AAUG) was established in Chicago by a group of Arab-
American professionals in the United States and Canada.
Its objectives are: 1. To establishe links among Arab-
Amricna professionals; 2. To cooperate with Arab-American colleagues for the purpose of promoting their professional activities and projects; 3. To utilize the
professional resources of Arab-Americans to make a contribution to our American community; 4. To disseminate
accurate scientific, cultural, and educational information and data about the Arab World among the AAUG membership and to the larger society; 5. To assist in
the development of the Arab World by providing the professional services of its membership where interests
of the latter and needs of the former coincide;
6. And through these various activities, to build
bridges of understanding and communications between
the two communities. Regular Membership is open to all
university graduates who are citizens or permanent residents of the United States, and who are of Arabic-
speaking origin. Associate and Student Membership
categories are open to anyone interested in Arab society and culture, and in fostering understanding between Arabs and Americans. It publishes the "AAUG Newsletter."

Dr. George Atiyeh became curator of the Arabic Section
of the Oriental Library, Library of Congress, Washington, D.C.

As a result of the June 1967 war, Mr. and Mrs. R. Bu-
sailah and Mr. and Mrs. W. Doering, all of Kokomo, Indiana organized Project Ryaiat (Loving Care). The Project gained the full support of the Greater Kokomo Association of Churches and the American-Arab Women's
Friendship Society of New York City. It is also sponsored by the Red Crescent Society of Jerusalem, a member of the League of Red Cross Societies. The aim of
the program is to gain sponsorship (on a $10 per month
basis) for children of Palestinian families which no
longer have a bread-winner.

The United American Arab Congress was founded in Los
Angeles. Its goals are to motivate the American-Arab
politically, to promote good relations between the
American and Arab peoples, and to explain to the American people the Palestinian problem. For these same
reasons, its members provide speakers and writers for
the media.

The International Arab Federation was founded by Joseph
Hayeck in Toledo. Its major aims are: to unite Americans of Arab origin; to promote the maintenance of
Arabic culture and language; to promote solidarity
among Arab-Americans to ensure their rights as an entity; and to advance and defend the Arab cause in the
USA. It publishes the Arab Tribune.

1968   Professor Fred J. Khouri of Villanova University pub-
            lished The Arab-Israeli Dilemma. The specialist will
            find the documentary support most useful.
            Woodrow W. Woody (Woody Shikany) of Mt. Clemens, Mich-
            igna, was honored with a papal appointment through the
            Maronite Exarch, Bishop Francis M. Zayek. Mr. Woody
            was invested as Knight Commander of the Holy Sepulchre
            of Jerusalem.

Nispols (Nick) N. Solomon was elected to the registry
of the International Who's Who for service to humanity and personal achievement. Mr. Solomon has served
on the staffs of the Attorney General of Louisiana and
the Governor of New Mexico.

Emile Khouri helped to design Disneyland.

On the June 5th anniversary of the Arab-Israeli War of
1967, Sirhan Bishara Sirhan, was accused of shooting
Senator Robert F. Kennedy following a political rally
in Los Angeles. Sirhan, a twenty-four-year-old Palestinian had been living in the Los Angeles area since
1957. He had permanent resident status. During the
trial which followed Sirhan was defended by court-ap-
pointed attorneys whom he chose from a list. The

prosecution and defense spent much time considering
the effect of Sirhan's broken home and his father's
desertion of the family as being responsible for Sirhan's crime. He was convicted and sentenced to life
imprisonment. During the subsequent appeals Sirhan's
defense was taken on by Arab-Amrican attorneys, Abdeen
Jabara and George Shibley who sought to point out the
political motivation behind the crime, and the effect
that Kennedy's compaigning to win the Jewish vote had
on this young Palestinian Christian who had vague memories of life in his occupied country. It was not Jabara's nor Shibley's aim in any way to diminish the
significance of the crime, but rather to put it in a
more accurate perspective for consideration by the A-
merican people.

The Holy Land Fund was organized in Chicago with the
purpose of "ameliorating the conditions of the people
of the Holy Land, particularly those who have been
affected by the present emotional, social and economic
instabilities characteristic of the region..."The United Holy Land Fund caters to the needs of the orphan,
the widow, the handicapped, the injured and the unskilled. The primary recipient of United Holy Land
Funds has been the Palestine Red Crescent Society, a
member of the International Red Cross. During the
years 1970, 1973, and 1976 over seven million dollars
worth of medical supplies alone were shipped to the
Palestine Red Crescent Society. The organization's
first president was Mr. Ahmad Issa, followed by Mr.
Rafat Rabi, Mr. Ihsan Diab and Mr. Mahmoud A. Naji.

November. Three American citizens of Yemeni origin w
were arrested and placed on $100,000 bond by Destrict
Attorney Golden in Brooklyn, New York. The three men,
Ahmed Namer, age 43, and his sons Husseion, age 20,
and Abdo, age 16, were charged with conspiring to
assassinate President Nixon, and possession of weapons
and dangerous instruments. The arrest was made on the
basis of a telephone tip by another Yemeni, Mohammed
Hazan Aljamal, who had lived in the Namer's apartment
from May to October of 1968, and whom he evicted when
Aljamal set fire to his bed with a lighted cigarette.
Aljamal had also been warned by Namer about his drunk-
eness, which Namer considered a serious breach of Islamic principle. Ambassador Alaini of Yemen said in
an interview regarding the arrests that there were
perhaps 5,000 or more Yemeni in the United States, both
those of American citizenship and those who were still
aliens. The Ambassador said that he did not believe
the Yemenis were involved in any plot. He explained
that in Yemen "everyone has arms. It is permitted."

The weapons found in the Namer apartment included
two rifles (an M-1 carbine with two clips of ammu-
nition and one conventional rifle with twenty-four
rounds) and two switchblade knives.

1969 July. An all-male State Supreme Court jury found
Ahmed, Hussein and Abdo Namer guilty of possession
of two switch blade knives and innocent on all other
counts.. Whereas the accusation of the Arab-Americans
of plotting to assassination of President Nixon appeared on page one of the <u>New York Times</u>, their acq-
uittal of the charge appeared on page seven. Mr.
Namer testified that he had purchased the two rifles
to give to relatives in Yemen where he had planned
to go in December, 1968. The judge reminded the
jury that possession of a rifle is not a crime unless
it is proved that there is intent to use it against
another person. The entire case had been based on
the testimony of Aljamal, which was subsequently
found to have no basis whatever in fact.

September. The National Federation of Syrian and
Lebanese Clubs at its annual convention honored the
following Arab-Americans with the "Arabic National
Achievement Award": Dr. Michael DeBakey, Najeeb Hal-
aby, Lt. Governor Elias Francis (New Mexico), Ralph
Nader, Gabriel Ofiesh, Alex Shoofey, Danny Thomas and
Mike Tamer.

The First Muslim-World Department was organized by
Dr. Abdulmunim Shakir at Picker College, a 126-year-
old liberal arts institution in Houlton, Maine.
Funding for the program was sought and received from
King Feisal of Saudi Arabia, the Arabian American
Oil Company and the government of Kuwait. Dr. Shakir,
himself a product for the Muslim world who is now an
American citizen, teaches courses in Arabic language,
Islamic institutions and culture. Dr. Shakir had the
encouragement and support of former Picker president,
Dr. C. Worth Howard, who for more than thirty years
had been a faculty member or acting president of the
American University of Cairo.

Dr. Nadeem M. Muna, head of the Microbiological
Science, Inc., in Salt Lake City, Utah, reported the
development of a simple blood test for melonoma.
This development holds promise of mass screening for
some other forms of cancer. Dr. Muna said that the
new development calls for only a sample of blood instead of conventional surgery biopsy and can be done
in the physician's office.

Mrs. Victor Estfan, who immigrated to the United

States in 1912 was awarded the title "Manchester Citizen of the Year" by the Greater Manchester, New
Hampshire Chamber of Commerce. Mrs. Esftan was cited
as having "Dedicated more than a half century of her
life in an unceasing effort to assist other immigrants."

The Arabic - speaking community in Patterson, New
Jersey, sponsored an Arabic picnic (mahrajan) which
attracted nearly 3,500 Arab - Americans from all over
the Northeast. The most significant aspect of this
particular "mahrajan" was that it was sponsored co-
operatively by the Melkite, Syrian Orthodox, and
Armenian - rite Catholic churches of Patterson.

> (See document No. 25)

Action newspaper began publication as the organ of
the Action Committee on American-Arab relations. Its
masthead quoted Jefferson's words, "I have sworn upon
the altar of God, eternal hostility against every
form of tyranny over the mind of man." The first editorial, spelling out the goal and philosophy of
the paper, was titled "To liberate the human mind
from prejudice and to liberate Palestine". In June
1974, the offices of Action Newspaper were burned in
a fire that the New York City Fire Marshall declared
had been deliberately set.

> (See document No. 51)

Al-Bayan newspaper became Action-Al-Bayan, eight
pages in English and, eight pages in Arabic. After
Raji Daher returned from a visit to Lebanon, he began publishing Al-Bayan from Detroit along with Nah-
dhat al-Arab. Action newspaper continued its publication in New York, as the organ of the Action Committee on American-Arab Relations, with Dr. M.T.
Mehdi as its executive editor.

Dr. Farouk El-Baz, Egyptian-born American, was the
"king" to whom the Apollo astronauts were referring
when from the moon they radioed "Tell the King we're
bringing him something from that little crater."
El-Baz, a geogolist, was one member of the team which
chose the landing sites on the moon. Now with the
National Air and Space Museum of the Smithsonian Institution in Washington, D.C., he is engaged in eval-
uating the scientific findings from the Apollo Missions. In keeping with the tradition of naming the
moon craters after those of the past who have contributed to science, Dr. El-Baz has named an area
"Necho" in honor of the Egyptian pharaoh who launched
a naval expedition to prove that Africa was surrounded
by water.

1970   Dr. Laura Nader, one of only fifteen women who are
            full professors at the University of California, Berk-
            eley, was pressing an aggressive campaign for law re-
            form, writing magazine articles and acadmeic papers
            and making speeches all urging a major overhaul in the
            workings of United States justice. When asked about
            the family that produced such remarkable people as
            Laura and Ralph Nader, Laura replied that her father,
            Nathra Nader retired restraunteur of Winsted, Connect-
            icut, kept the focus on "important considerations".
            Even at the dinner table, she said, "We sure didn't
            sit around talking about the weather."

            Under the leadership of the Rev. Archimandrite Gregory
            Abboud, St. Nicholas Cathedral in Brooklyn, New York,
            purchased land on Staten Island and instituted plans
            for the construction of a Home for the Aged. The Home
            is to be dedicated to all of the Arabic - speaking
            people in North America and those related to them,
            regardless of their religious beliefs.

            A thirteen year old Arab-American boy from Ramsey,
            New Jersey, received the "In the Name of God Award"
            for the Islamic faith in an Eagle Scout ceremony.
            It was the first time the award had been present-
            ed to a Moslem scout in the Eastern United States.

            Dr. William A. Small of Geneseo, New York, was re-elec-
            ted president of the Federated American-Arab Organiza-
            tions at its annual three-day conference in New York
            City.

            Jerrier Abdo Haddad, son of journalist Abdulmassih
            Haddad, led the engineering team that developed the
            first IBM electronic calculator which was mass produced.

            Paul Anka's career as singer-composer continued as he
            produced hits such as "Diana," "I'm Just a Lonely Boy,"
            "My Shoulder," and "My Way."

            Salemeh Hassen operated as trainer to Mohammed Ali.

            All religious segments of the Arab-American community,
            Christian and Moslem - joined together in the Washing-
            ton Cathedral, Washington, D.C., in a "Plea for Justice
            for People of the Holy Land." Dr. Frank Maria, Chair-
            man of the Department of Near East and Arab Refugee
            Problems for the Antiochian Orthodox Church of North
            America was program director of the meeting. An Inter-
            national Festival honoring Arab-American writer and

An International Festival honoring Arab-American writer and artist Khalil Gibran was held at the American University of Beirut, Lebanon.

"Quick thinking and quick action" were the words _Time_ Magazine used to describe New York City police detective James M. Zeide who saved the life of Chiang Ching-Kuo, son of Chiang Kai-Sheck, when pursued by an assassin at a meeting at the Far East-America Council for Commerce and Industry at the Plaza Hotel. Detective Zeide received thanks from both the State Department and President Nixon.

Yusuf A. Najem, Arab-American writer, died.

The American University of Beirut (Syrian Protestant College until 1921) celebrated its 100 year anniversary.

The Canadian-Arab Review began publication in Montreal, Canada. The Review, which is issued in three languages-Arabic, English, and French - is edited by Mr. Raymond Kneider and emphasizes news of the Canadian-Arab community, Arab culture, politics, and tourism in the Arab World.

A delegation from the Federated Organizations on American-Arab Relations met with the legislative staff of Senator Mark Harfield (R-Oregon) at the Senate Office Building to express appreciation for the Senator's statement on the floor of the Senate concerning the Middle East. Senator Hatfield had stated that the Palestinians must be considered in any solution to the Mid East conflict. Members of the delegation from the Federated Organizations included M.G. Sadak, President of the Washington Chapter of the World Lebanese Union, Nabil Awad, John Asha, Joe Samaha and M.T. Mehdi.

The American-Arab Association of Lehigh Valley, Pennsylvania, announced the translation of its constitution into Arabic. The announcement was made by Albert Attieh, vice president of the Association. Other officers include Nasim Wachim, president, Suheil Barber, treasurer, and Kamal Abboud, secretary.

St. Nicholas Antiochian Orthodox Cathedral in Brooklyn, New York, celebrated its fiftieth anniversary. Father Gregory Abboud, pastor of St. Nicholas used the occasion to thank the ladies Aid Society, the Ladies of Hamelat El Teeb, the St. Nicholas Young Men's Association, St. Mary's Orthodox church in Brooklyn and a

number of individual friends and members of the
Cathedral for their generous contributions toward
the St. Nicholas Home for the Aged being constructed
on Staten Island. Mr. Richard Zraick served as
chairman of the Souvenier Journal and of the banquet.

William Nahas of New London, Connecticut was elected
mayor of the city.

Dr. Charles Homra of Murray State University, Murray,
Kentucky, was selected to have his name appear in the
1970 edition of Outstanding Educators of America.

1971

August. Dr. Muhsin Mahdi, president of the Society
for the Study of Islamic Philosophy and Science, addressed the first world-wide meeting of the Society
which was held at Columbia University. Dr. Mahdi, a
native of Iraq,is the Director of the Harvard Middle
East Studies Center.

September. The Forum for Arab Art and Culture sponsored a much-heralded tour of the United States for
famed Lebanese singer, Feyrouz and her troupe of
sixty Dabke dancers and musicians from Baalbeck. President Nixon is quoted to have said that he was greatly
pleased that America would have the opportunity to hear
Lebanon's greatest singer. The tour began at Carnegie
Hall in New York City and concluded in San Francisco.

Mr. Michael Nackel, president of the American-Arabic
Association of Boston, Massachusetts, submitted a
three page statement on the question of the Holy City
of Jerusalem at the request of the House of Repres-
sentatives' Foreign Relations Committee.

Dr. Fouad Al Akl noted Arab-American surgeon and poet
died. Dr. Al Akl who wrote a number of definitive
texts in the fields of surgery was a founder of the
Salaam club, American Middle East Relief and the American Academy of Poetry. His autobiographical insights
are collected in Until Summer Comes.

Sabah P. Najor of Detroit was appointed interim Secretary of State for the state of Michigan.

Dr. Alexander A. Kirkish was elected by the Western
Federation of Syrian-Lebanese American Clubs as "Man
of the Year".

Marlo Thomas of "That Girl" television fame spurred
efforts of the ALSAC (American Lebanese Syrian Associated Charities) to raise money for St. Jude Hospital
in Memphis, Tennessee, the Philathrophic creation of
her father, Arab-American comedian, Danny Thomas.
Working with Marlo Thomas was ALSAC Vice-President,
Jim Maloof, Regional Director, Ethel Bekolay, and
Major Al Toler. An outstanding feature of ALSAC's
fund-raising for St. Jude has always been the Teenagers
March.

It appeared that Al Hoda the oldest Arabic language
newspaper in the United States would be closing.
However, Fares Stephan, of Stephan's Travel Agency,
purchased the paper and pledged to continue it with
the dean of Arab journalism, Fred Khoury, still active
as editor.

The "Baylor College of Medicine - Dr. Michael DeBakey
Fund" was established with a grant from the southern
Federation of Syrian Lebanese American Clubs. It
was announced that Dr. DeBakey would head the project.

George Alexander Doumani reached the South Pole and
had a mountain peak there named after him. Doumani
is a staff member of the Science Policy Research Division of the Congressional Research Service of the
Library of Congress. He is an active proponent of
the theory of 'continental drift" and a leading geologist, glaciologist, and oceanographer.

William Peter Blatty published The Exorcist, the
screenplay of which won him an Academy Award. The
book was translated into German, Spanish, Italian,
French, Greek, Hebrew, Turkish and Japanese.

1972   Major George Jowan served as assistant to presidential
            aide, General Alexander Haig.

"Operation Boulder" or the "Special Measures" were
instituted by the Nixon administration. Designed,
it was said, to combat "terrorism" in the United
States, the thrust of this operation was against "ethnic Arabs" who were so defined on the basis of a person's parentage. The Arab-American community took
strong exception to this type of operation, and considerable correspondence took place between leaders
of the Arab-American legal community and the federal
government.

(See documents No. 45, No. 46, and No. 47)

The Greater Cleveland Council on Arab-American Relations was founded. Its first president was Minor
George. The GCAAA was not begun by a special religious
or fraternal group, but was the coming together of
Greater Clevelanders of Arabic descent without regard
to national origin, religious affiliation or political
preference. In 1976 the organization became a chapter
of the National Association of Arab-Americans and
changed its name to the Greater Cleveland Association
of Arab-Americans. It represents Cleveland's 25,000
Arab-Americans and its major activities include pre-
senting cultural programs about the Arab world, com-
municating with legislators, providing that speakers
for groups interested in Arab-Americans or the Middle
East, and supporting candidates for political office.

Dr. M.T. Mehdi appeared on the Dick Cavett Show to
respond to anti-Arab remarks made on a previous show
by Senator Jacob Javits and Otto Preminger.

The Al-Islah Arabic newspaper celebrated its fortieth
anniversary. Its editor and publisher, Dr. J. Alphonse
Chaurize, said that he, as well as the editors of
other Arabic papers, have been serving the Arabic
language and preserving it in Al-Mahjar (land of the
immigrants). Despite the difficulties and high cost
of printing in New York, Dr. Chaurize said he was determined to continue serving the Arab-American community and the "beautiful language that we love."

Mr. Omar Ghobashi, prominent Arab-American lawyer,
who is an authority on the American Indians and has
defended many of the tribes in New York against the
state and the federal government, was active in de-
fending numerous Arabs before the Immigration Department. Ghobashi has also written extensively
about Indian tribal land rights.

Four hundred members of the American Arab Society and
several representatives of the American Arab Chamber
of Commerce gathered at Gleannloch owned by Douglas
B. Marshall, the founder and life-time honorary president of the Society. The occasion was the seventh
anniversary of the American Arab Society, whose current president Ahmed Rahman reviewed activities of
the Society which in 1968 established the American
Arab Chamber of Commerce as an independent affiliate.
Dr. Atef Gamal-Eldin, the Chamber's Secretary-General
was also present.

Toby Moffett was elected United States Congressman
from Conneticut. Moffett is the son of Anton Hanna
Mahfouz and began his government career as the first

Director of the Office of Students and Youth for the
federal government. In 1971 he accepted an offer from
Ralph Nader to become the first director of the Connecticut Citizen Action Group. Moffett was praised
in Eric Redman's The Dance of Legislation as knowing
that "political effectiveness demands hard work, self-
discipline, ingenuity and pragmatism."

George R. Simon, Chicago businessman, and Phyllis Joseph, Cleveland schoolteacher, were honored as the Man
and Woman of the year by the Midwest Federation of
American Syrian-Lebanese Clubs at their annual convention in Milwaukee, Wisconsin.

Thirty-five students were announced as winners of the
R.G. Haddad Foundation scholarship awards. The Samra
Memorial Award of $500 went to Ellen Marie Marshall of
Canton, Massachusetts, a sociology major at Northwestern
University.

The Moslem community of Cedar Rapids, Iowa dedicated
a new mosque and Islamic Center five times larger
than the existing mosque. The new Center contains
in addition to a prayer hall, a small school and library. The new complex which costs $150,000 was fi-
nanced entirely from local funds. Abdullah Igram was
chairman of the Dedication Committee.

The Arab American Social Cultural Club opened its
headquarters on Atlantic Avenue in Brooklyn. Officers
included: Amin Awad president of the Club, Subhi
Al Waddi, vice president; Mohammad Massoud, treasurer.
Naif Hassan Hamdan, assistant treasurer; and Dr. Omar
Ghobashi, legal advisor.

The American Association of Teachers of Arabic published its spring journal "An Nashra", wherein they
stated that the enrollment in Arabic language courses
in the United States had risen from 541 in 1960 to
1,669 in 1972.

Metropolitan Michael Shaheen of Toledo, announced
plans to break grounds for the new St. George Anti-
ochian Orthodox Cathedral of Toledo, Ohio, considered
Phase One of the proposed million-dollar Orthodox
Center for Toledo, Ohio. Ground-breaking ceremonies
were held on April 23, 1972. Co-Chairman of the
Phase One project were Richard O. Joseph and Michael
Damas, both of Toledo, and president of the Board of
Trustees was George M. Saba. The Pastor of the
Cathedral is Rev. Mark Pemberton.

Salah Mourad began publication of Mougaz-El-Anbaa

(The News in Brief). This weekly magazine primarily
covers news of Egypt and serves the Egyptian-American
community.

Arabic calligraphy took the spotlight at the Arab World
Booth at the International Fair in Boston, Massachusetts,
as people waited in line to have their names written
in Arabic. Old and young alike were fascinated to
watch their names take on artistic proportions as
George Mudarri and Ali Abu-Hasan wrote them out. Those
who waited in line had an opportunity to examine the
beautiful handpainted calligraphic mottos done by
Mudarri to benefit the American Arabic Association.
Evelyn Menconi of Dorchester, Massachusetts has compiled a book to help children learn more about the
development of the alphabet which had its birth in
the Arab World.

Laurice Peters of Parma, Ohio, continued to appear
on programs of the Arab-American communities across
the United States. Her repertoire of both traditional
and contemporary Arabic songs has made her a perrenial
favorite. Her latest recording, "Gibran", echoes in
song the words of the great Arab-American poet.

Dr. M. Cherif Bassiouni, Prof. of International Law
at DePaul University appeared on the "Today Show."
Abraham Kazen, Jr., of Laredo, Texas was re-elected
to his fourth term in the United States House of Representatives. Kazen commented that his district in
Texas covers 17,384 square miles or about four times
the area of Lebanon, the birthplace of his father.

Arabesque Radio under producer and director Ghazi
Khankan celebrated its fifth year on WHBI New York.

1973   James Abdnor was elected United States Congressman
from South Dakota. Abdnor's interest in politics
had already seen him serve as State Senator and
Lieutenant Governor of the state. His parents had immigrated from Lebanon, and Sam Abdnor, his father,
had peddled dry goods by horse and wagon through
parts of Nebraska, Minnesota, Kansas and South Dakota.
Abdnor makes his home in Kennebec, South Dakota.
His congressional assignments have included the Public
Works Committee and the Committee on Veterans Affairs.

Samuel Hazo's book of poetry, Once For the Last Ban-
dit, was nominated by the National Book Award Committee
for being one of the best books of 1973.

The American - Ramallah Federation held its 15th Annual Convention. Some 2,000 members attended. Members

of the Federation are immigrants from the village of
Ramallah and their descendants.

August. Naji Daifullah, a Yemeni immigrant and member
of the United Farm Workers Union was killed, along
with co-worker Juan de la Cruz, during a union protest
in Lamont, California. Caesar Chavez said of Naji,
he often served as an interpreter at union functions
and gave himself fully to the grape strike and the
assertion for farm worker justice."

(See document No. 53)

October. When war broke out in the Middle East, the
Arab-American workers in Detroit, Michigan's auto industry had a demonstration supported by a coalition
of Arab organizations in the city. Nearly 2,000
workers took the day off to protest the United Auto
Workers union purchase of Israeli Bonds.

The Rt. Rev. Archimandrite Alexander George, pastor
of St. John's Eastern Orthodox Archidiocese of Toledo,
Ohio was appointed coordinator for a new program for
the rehabilitation of first-offense drunk drivers in
seven eastern Iowa countries. The Iowa Legislature
passed a Law making the rehabilitation program man-
datory, and the governor of Iowa appointed Rev. George
to coordinate the program at Kirkwood College in Cedar
Rapids.

The seventy-fifth anniversary of the Arabic language
newspaper, Al-Hoda, was held at the Waldorf Astoria
Hotel in New York City. Mr. Edward A. Zraick served
as chairman of the Jubilee Committee. Al Hoda is the
oldest, continually published Arabic language newspaper in the United States.

Tige Andrews was seen weekly on T.V. as the detective
on "Mod Squad".

The National Association of Arab - Americans (N.A.A.A.)
was founded to act as a political lobby in Washington
on behalf of Arab - Americans. The goals were to encourage Arab - Americans' political participation
(especially by running for office), and to promote a
more "even-handed" Middle East policy. It was the beginning of the "Arabization" of the Syrians, Lebanese, etc. The first president of the organization
was Dr. Peter Tanous.

(See document No. 49 and No. 50)

1974   Dr. Philip Habib became Assistant Secretary of State
for East Asian and Pacific Affairs. As a foreign service officer Dr. Habib had previously served the

United States government in Canada, New Zealand, Port
of Spain, Seoul, Saigon, Paris and Korea.

William J. Baroody, Jr. was appointed by President
Ford as Assistant to the President in charge of the
Office of Public Liason. Mr. Baroody had previously
served in the Department of Defense and in a staff
capacity in Congress.

The Arab American Medical Association was founded.
Its objectives are to provide medical aid to the
needy in the Middle East and to Arab-Americans; to
provide scholarships for needy medical students of
Arabic heritage; to enhance medical knowledge; to promote medical relations between its members who share
common background; to perpetuate the pride of heritage; to be a medical host unit and to help newly
graduated medical students.

James Abourezk was elected United States Senator from
South Dakota. In 1970 he had been elected the first
Democrat in thirty-six years from South Dakota's Second Congressional District. Senator Abourezk's father
had immigrated to the United States from Lebanon in
1895 and worked as a pack-peddler until 1910 when
he brought his own store in Wood, South Dakota, which
at that time was part of the Rosebud Sioux Indian
Reservation. The senator grew up in the area, received
his law degree from the University of South Dakota
School of Law and then established his home and practice in Rapid City. During his years in the House of
Representatives, Abourezk authorized the Family Farm
Act of 1972, the National Power Grid Act, and Amend-
ments to the 1970 Disaster Relief Act. Senator Abour-
izk was assigned to the Committee on Aeronautics and
Space Sciences, the Committee on the Interior and Insular Affairs, and the Select Committee on Small Business Administration. He has played an active role
in portraying the plight of the Palestinians to the
U.S. Congress and in stressing the need for the United
States to play an active role in the peacemaking pro-
cedures in the Middle East.

Helen Thomas was designated by United Press International as its White House reporter. Thomas was the
first woman to head the Presidential reporting team
of a major news service. A veteran of thirty years
of Washington reporting, Thomas has been on the White
House beat for fourteen years.

The third annual Arab World Festival held in Detroit
brought together 250,000 Arab-Americans to enjoy Arabic
food, listen and dance to Arabic music, watch Alex
Acie, at 64 perform the ritual Arab sword dance, and
enjoy the comraderie of some twenty-eight Arab clubs
in Detroit.

Joseph Robbie, managing general partner of the Miami
Dolphins, saw his team win the second super Bowl in
a row.

Edward Hanna was elected mayor of Utica, New York.
He quickly acquired the reputation of being unique
in city government. Hanna, who has lived in Utica
all his life, became New York's first Independent May-
or since 1885. He has been described as being "hyper-
actively immersed in his 'People's Government' by
managing five of the city's departments, besides his
own." Hanna accepts only $1.00 of his $20,000 salary,
and he had had the doors removed from his office to
make himself more available to the people of his city.
Prior to his election as mayor, Hanna served a term
in the New York State Assembly.

In an interview with the <u>Christian Science Monitor</u>,
Halim El-Dabh, Professor of Ethnomusicology at Kent
State University in Ohio, was described as a "compos-
er of remarkable insight and boldness". Professor
El-Dabh spent many years studying the ancient music
of the Coptic Church. He was chosen by the Egyptian
Cultural Ministry to write the "Son et Lumiere" music
for the Pyramids. Professor El-Dabh lived for a per-
iod in the tombs at Abu Simbel where he discovered
paintings of harp orchestras and wind instruments,
including the clarinet which originated in ancient
Egypt. During thirty years of study in Africa, El-
Dabh also lived in Senegal, Mali, and with the Taurez.
Recordings he made are now housed in the Library of
Congress.

Gamal El-Zoghby, Egyptian-born interior-architect, was
voted one of the top ten designers in the U.S. by
<u>Progressive Architecture Magazine</u>.

The Arabic-speaking community of Detorit, Michigan was
judged to be sufficiently large for Town Pride, Associated Food Distributors, Inc. to begin printing their
canned food lables in the Arabic language as well as
English.

The Arab Athletic Club soccer team became Third Division leaders in San Francisco.

Michael J. Thomas, sports writer for the Providence, Rhode Island Journal Bulletin, died on January 2. Thomas was generally credited with "discovering" boxer Rocky Marciano, former world heavyweight champion.

The monthly newsletter of the National Association of Arab-Americans, "The Voice", made its debut.

Joseph J. Rookis of Birmingham, Alabama, was cited as instrumental in the establishment of the only Diabetes Research and Education Hospital in the entire world. It is located in Birmingham.

Stage and screen star, Paul Jabara, appeared on Movie of the Week, "The Last Angry Man" on ABC-TV.

The American Arabic Speaking Community Almanac for 1974 was published by Joseph R. Haiek, editor and publisher of The News Circle.

The Federated-Arab-American Organizations commemorated the 25th Anniversary of the Dier Yassin massacre with a memorial service at the Church Center for the United Nations, New York City. Dr. William Small, president of the Federation, presided.

Chuck Nader of Gardena, California, was victorious in the City Council election.

Richard Kotite was promoted to the rank of general in the United States Army. For his distinguished service, he has received the Purple Heart, the Bronze Star, the Commanding Ribbon, and the Service Cross.

Khalid S. M. Al-Najdi (known in the entertainment world as Ali Baba) was the first Kuwaiti to become an American citizen.

The American Syrian Lebanese community honored Bill George, the one-time middle linebacker of the Chicago Bears. The testimonial was held one day after George's induction into the Pro Football Hall of Fame.

The memory of World War II hero, Corporal Raymond A.L. Saquet, was honored in the dedication of a square in Boston, Massachusetts.

U.S. Senator James Abourezk was named by <u>Time</u> maga-
zine as Young American Leader in its article "200
Faces for the Future." Also named by <u>Time</u> were A.
Robert Abboud, Deputy Chairman of the First Chicago
Corporation, and Ralph Nader consumer advocate.

The Michael Berry International Terminal, which services all international carriers through Detroit, was
the first to be named after a person of Arab heritage.
Berry, a Dearborn attorney, had worked zealously for
a multi-million dollar airport expansion program and
saw this as tripling international air travel in the
Detroit area.

Victor R. Kattak, Director of the New Jersey Arabic
Cultural Institute, announced the establishment of
the Institute at St. Ann's Melkite Catholic Education
Center in West Patterson, New Jersey.

The R.G. Haddad Foundation issued grants to thirty-
five college-bound men and women of Syrian or Lebanese descent. Dr. John Dalack, president, stated that
the value of the awards totaled $14,100.

The Jeanette, Pennsylvania, commissioners declared
September 15th. "Monsour Day" in Westmoreland County.
Mr. and Mrs. Nadra Nader, parents of consumer advocate,
Ralph Nader and University of California anthropology
professor, Dr. Laura Nader, attended Monsour Day along
with 1200 others.

National Association of Arab-American officers,
Richard C. Shadyac, president, Peter S. Tanous,
past president, and Edmond Howar, vice-president,
were guests at a State Department dinner hosted
by Secretary of State, Henry Kissinger.

Mrs. Samira Zara Al-Quazzaz was elected president of
U.S. OMEN for 1975, becoming the first woman to hold
that position.

Over 1.700 delegated from over twenty-five cities across the United States and Canada rallied in downtown
Manhattan on November 13, to welcome the Palestine
Liberation Organization (PLO) to the United Nations
in New York. The invitation to Yassir Arafat to address the General Assembly of the U.N. brought an out-
pouring of support from Arab-American communities
across the country.

A delegation of Arab-Americans, headed by Mrs. Marg-
aret Pennar visited Angier Biddle Duke, Chairman of
the Council on Inter-Community Affairs of New York
City to draw his attention to the fact that Arab-Americans have been the victims of violent crimes perpet-
rated by federal agencies. As a result of the meeting,
Arab-Americans were asked to be represented for the
first time on the Inter-Community Advisory Council
of New York.

1975   The Board of Directors of the Arab-Cultural Center
            of San Francisco announced the purchase of a twelve-
            room mansion which will house the various Arab-Ameri-
            can organizations in the Bay Area and which will hold
            functions and activities to promote Arabic culture.
            The San Francisco Arab Cultural Center is the first
            of its kind in the United States. In its Newsletter
            the Board of Directors said, "We must emphasize here
            that the new center was built by the community's money.
            This important fact proved beyond any doubt that our
            community can achieve miracles when united and working
            together for one common goal."

            A detailed analysis of the treatment of the Arabs in
            elementary and junior high school textbooks was made
            for the California State Board of Education. The
            study entitled, "The Arabs in American Textbooks,"
            was conducted by Dr. Ayad Al-Quazzaz, Assoicate Pro-
            fessor of Sociology, California State University at
            Sacramento and Ruth Afifi, Jean Pelletiere and Audrey
            Shabbas, emebers of NAJDA (Women Concerned About the
            Middle East.)

            Mahmud Thamer, M.D. from Najef, Iraq, began teaching
            cardiology at Johns Hopkins Medical School.

            Mohammad Haki heads the public affairs office of the
            World Bank.

            Adel Assad Yunis, M.D., chief of hematology at the
            University of Miami School of Medicine, isolated a
            substance in cancer cells that destroys fibrin, the
            protein that makes possible the clotting of blood.

            Sami A. Hashim, director of the laboratory for nutri-
            tion and metabolism at St. Luke's Hospital Center,
            New York, has published more than 150 articlaes as a
            result of his research.

The truck industry of Detroit is benefitting from Joseph Simon's development of a cold-form process for making truck-axel spindles which gives greater strength at lower cost.

Anthony R. Abraham of Miami, Florida, is president of the World Lebanese Cultural Union while carrying on a business which bills him as the world's largest Chevrolet dealer.

Thomas L. Hazouri was the second Arab-American to be serving in the Florida State Legislature. At the age of 31 he won his seat in the Florida House. Prior to his election Hazouri worked as executive assistant to the Majority Leader in the Florida House of Representatives, and prior to that he worked as information and research assistant to the mayor of Jacksonville, his home town.

James J. Tayoun was elected to the Pennsylvania House of Representatives. He also represented his Philadelphia district in the House in 1969-70 and 1973-74. Mr. Tayoun has been active in the field of mental health programming serves on the board of the International YMCA.

The American-Arab Association for Commerce and Industry, Inc. reported that combined United States-Arab trade for the year stood at $12 billion. The organization was founded by a group of American businessmen in 1951 when total trade stood at $440 million.

Mansour Alwan was elected mayor of Chesilhurst, New Jersey. Alwan had previously been appointed to serve the unexpired term of the previous mayor.

The two Syrian Orthodox Archdioceses joined to become the Antiochian Archdiocese of North America.

The "Islamic Council" was established. It was to be the umbrella organization for all Moslems in New England.

CBS presented its first documentary on Arab-Americans, featuring the Arab-American community in Southern California.

Faculties of many American colleges and universities were sharing the expertise of Arab-American scholars, To name just a few:

Majid Khadduri, Johns Hopkins School of Advanced
   International Studies
Aziz S. Atiya, University of Utah
Charles P. Issawi, Princeton University
Muhsin Mahdi, Harvard University
Edward Said, Columbia University
Abdo A. Elkholy, Northern Illinois University
Adele Younis, Salem State College
Elaine Hagopian, Simmons College
Michael Suleiman, University of Kansas
M. Cherif Bassiouni, De Paul University
Hisham Sharabi, Georgetown University
Ismael Faruqi, Temple University
Ibrahim Abu-Lughod, Northwestern University
Barbara Aswad, Wayne State University
Abdul Karim Khudairi, Northeastern University
Caesar Farah, University of Minnesota
Philip M Kayal, Seton Hall University

Richard Elias, M.D. and Eugene Sayfie, M.D., both well-
known cardiologists were sharing their expertise with
the Miami Heart Institute, Miami, Florida.

Raji Daher, editor and publisher of Al-Bayan retired
to Phoenix, Ariz ona. Al-Bayan had maintained throughout its long history the reputation as an Arab-American newspaper of the very highest intellectual and
literary quality.

1976   Dr. George E. Assousa, staff member in astrophysics
            at the Department of Terrestrial Magnetism of the
            Carnegie Institution of Washington, D.C., coordinated
            the first meeting of Arab physicists in the U.S. and
            Canada in Washington, D.C.

Tewfiq Zayyad, mayor of Nazareth, Dr. Emile Touma, editor of the largest Arab-Israeli daily, al-Ittihad
("Unity") and Mrs. Felicia Langer, Israeli lawyer and
author of With My Own Eyes were featured speakers at
the ninth annual convention of the Association of
Arab-American University Graduates in New York City.
Following the convention, the three speakers appeared
before audiences in San Francisco, Chicago, Los Angeles,
Washington and Boston.

Danny Thomas and the St. Jude Children's Research Institute presented Arab-American Paul Anka in a concert.
Paul Anka has written over 400 songs. At the age of
fifteen his first record "Diana" established him as
a million-selling record artist. Anka also wrote the
theme music for the "Johnny Carson Show."

Vance Bourjaily published <u>Now Playing at Canterbury</u>.
This had been preceeded by such former works as
<u>Confessions of a Spent Youth</u> and <u>The Man Who Knew</u>
<u>Kennedy</u>.

Mary Rose Oakar from Cleveland, Ohio, became the first
Arab-American Congresswoman. Oakar won a decisive
election in Ohio's 20th District.

Herb Macol was elected mayor of Mankato, Minnesota.

Mustafa Akkad, Los Angeles film producer, completed
his epic film, "Mohammad, Messenger of God." The
film opened in the United States in 1977 and has among
its roster of stars Arab-American, Michael Ansara.

A report titled "Incorporating An Awaremess of the
Arab World into the American Educational Ecperience"
was issued by Denoyer Geppert Publishers as a result
of a conference held on that topic in Chicago on
August 3rd. Among the educators present were Arab-
American Sameera Hennein and Mary Al-Azzawi.

The Action Committee on American-Arab Relations changed
its name to the American-Arab Relations Committee(AARC).

<u>Action</u> English-Arabic Newspaper resumed publication
in New York City. Publication had been suspended
since arsonists had burned the offices of the paper
in June, 1974.

<u>The Prophet</u>, by Kahlil Gibran, sold well over four
million copies. In one week of June alone, over 5,000
copies of the mini-volume were sold. Gibran has out-
sold all American poets. Stefan Kanfer, in the <u>New</u>
<u>York Times</u>, June 25, 1972, tried to belittle <u>The</u>
<u>Prophet</u> but had to admit that the book "has stared
at me from Army footlockers, from desks when I crammed
at N.Y.U., lectured at Columbia, taught at C.U.N.Y.
It followed me when I strolled the yards and quads
at Emory, Chicago, Harvard, Miami, Bennington, Washington and yes, by the beard cf the prophet, at Cam-
bridge, Heidelberg and the Sorbonne."

Large numbers of Arab-Americans participated in the
international conferences which took place in Tripoli,
Libya, and Baghdad, Iraq.

The civil war in Lebanon divided the Arab community
in America. There were "right wing" Lebanese demonstrations against the United Nations and "left wing"
demonstrations against Syrian intervention in Lebanon.

The United States Information Agency made a feature
film about five Arab-Americans and their success in
the United States. The five persons chosen to be so
honored were: Raymond Jallow, vice president of
United California Bank; Farouk El-Baz, geologist for
the Apollo Moon Landing; Joseph Robbie, principal
owner of the Miami Dolphina; Abdulmunim Shakir, dir-
ecotr of Muslim-World Studies at Ricker College, Houston, Maine; and George Simon, builder of factories
in Latin America from his base in Detroit.

Fred Haddad of Charleston, West Virginia saw Heck's
Inc., expand to include thirty-five discount department stores and sixty-five women's sportswear shops
stretching from Michigan to Florida.

Dale Shaheen of Williamson, West Virginia, formerly
a pilot with Middle East Airlines and now a prominent
businessman in Williamson, continued his active participation in efforts to better Arab-American relations in the Middle East.

Robert Rahall was elected to the United States Congress, as a representative of West Virginia.

N. Joe and Farris Rahall head Rahall Communications
Corporation, with radio stations in Beckley and Ind-
ianapolis, Indiana, Allentown, Pennsylvania, and St.
Petersburg, Florida.

A. Robert Abboud serves as vice chairman of the board
of the First Chicago Corporation.

Woodrow W. Woody, who emigrated to the United States
from Lebanon in 1912, becoming an emminently successful businessman in both Michigan and Florida, has
honored his parents' memory by building a school and
clinic in his native village of Bejderfel.

Fred Maroon's prize-winning photography continued to
appear in top national magazines.

Abe Gibron, the former pro-football star, served as
head coach of the Chicago Bears.

Lois DeBakey Ph.D., sister of the famed Dr. Michael
DeBakey, is professor of scientific communications
in the Department of Surgery at Baylor University.

George J. Mitchell is a ranking member of the National Committee of the Democratic Party in Maine. He
was active in Senator Edmund J. Muskie's presidential
campaign in 1972. He had made his own unsuccessful
try for governor of Maine in 1974.

Dr. M.T. Mehdi authored <u>Peace In Palestine</u> which was
published by New World Press, New York. It posed new
directions for American foreign policy in the Middle
East.

George A. Simon, together with his brother Joseph,
build and completely outfit factories for such clients
as Ford and Kaiser. Their projects have played a
large part in the industrialization of Latin America.

The Texas Haggar family name can be found on high
quality trousers sold around the world.

1977   His Holiness Pope Shenouda III, spiritual head of some
          85,000 Coptic Christians in North Aemrica toured the
          United States and Canada and met with President Carter
          to discuss the role of the Coptic Church in the United
          States. The Coptic Pope has his headquarters in Alex-
          andria, Egypt.

          Isa Sabbagh, an American of Palestinian origin, travel-
          ed as interpreter with President Carter to his meeting
          with Syrian President Hafez al-Assad in Geneva.

          At a convention of the Grocery Association of America,
          Paul Rand Dixon, a Federal Trade Commissioner, referred
          to Arab-American comsumer-advocate Ralph Nader as "a
          dirty Arab". The Arab-American community and its or-
          ganizations responded immediately to this ethnic slur,
          and the issue was taken up directly with the White
          House.

          (See documents No. 54 and No. 55)

          Arab-American Attorney, Robert W. Thabit, defended the
          United States-Arab Chamber of Commerce in a hearing
          before the New York State Human Rights Commission.

DOCUMENTS

DOCUMENT 1 - 1789

CORRESPONDENCE BETWEEN MOHAMMED III,
EMPEROR OF MOROCCO AND GEORGE WASHINGTON
PRESIDENT OF THE UNITED STATES
1788 and 1789

LETTER TO GEORGE WASHINGTON
FROM MOHAMMED III, EMPEROR OF MOROCCO
August 17, 1788

To the Great President of the United States of America, May
Peace be upon those who follow the paths of righteousness.

We have received your letter together with the Treaty of Peace
which you have addressed to us. We have written to Tunis and Tripoli regarding your request and all that you desire will be accom-
plished with God's will. May peace be upon you.

LETTER TO THE EMPEROR OF MOROCCO
PENNED IN GEORGE WASHINGTON'S OWN HAND
December 1, 1789

Great and magnaimous Friend,
    Since the date of the letter, which the late Congrefs, by
their President, addressed to your Imperial Majesty, the United
States of America, have thought proper to change their Government
and to institute a new one, agreeable to the Constitution, of
which I have the honor of herewith inclosing a Copy. The time nece-
fsarily employed in this arduous task, and the arrangements occa-
sioned by so great, though peaceable a Revolution, still apologise
and account for your Magesty's not having received those regular
advices, and marks of attention from the United States which the
Friendship and Magnaminity of your conduct towards them, afforded
warm to respect.
    The United States, having unanimously appointed me to the
Supreme executive authority in this nation your Majestys letter of
the 7th of August 1788 which, by reason of the disfolution of the
late Government, remained unanswered, has been delivered to me.
I have also received the letters, which your Imperial Majesty has
been so kind as to write, in favor of the United States, to the
Pashaws of Tunis and Tripoli, and I present to you the sincere ac-
knowledgements and thanks of the United States, for this important
mark of your friendship for them.
    We greatly regret that the hostile disposition of those regimes
towards this nation, who have never injured them, is not to be removed on terms in our power to comply with. Within our territories
there are no mines either of Gold or Silver, and this young Nation,
just recovering from the waste and defsolation of a long war, have
not, as yet, had time to acquire reches by agriculture and Commerce.
But our soil is bountiful, and our people industrious, and we have

reason to flatter ourselves that we shall gradually become useful to
our friends.

The encouragement which your Majesty has been pleased, generous-
ly, to give to our Commerce with your Dominions, the punctuality
with which you have caused the Treaty with us to be observed, and
the just and generous measures taken in the case of Captain Proctor,
make a deep imprefsion on the United States, and confirm their respect for, and attachment to your Imperial Majesty.

It gives me pleasure to have this opportunity of afsuring your
majesty that, while I remain at the head of this nation, I shall
not cease to promote every measure that may conduce to the Friendship
and Harmony which so happily subsist between your Empire and them...

In the course of the approaching winter, the national legislature (which is called by the former name of Congrefs) will afsemble,
and I shall take care that nothing be omitted that may necefsary to
cause the correspondence between our two countries to be maintained
and conducted in a manner agreeable to your majesty, and satisfactory to all the parties concerned in it.

May the Almighty blefs your Imperial Majesty
our great and magnanimour Friend, with his constant guidance
and protection. Written at the City of New York the first
day of December 1789.   G. Washington
To Our great and magnanimous Friend, His imperial majesty
     the Emperor of Morocco
                    (signed)   G. Washington

The Treaty of Friendship between Morocco and the United States was
renewed during the term of President Madison for a period of 50
years. When renewed again during the term of President Andrew
Jackson, a significant paragraph was added:

"This Treaty shall continue between the two countries in
accordance with valid rules until one party informs the
other of its intention to cancel it and this would be
effective one year later."

To this day, no party has notified the other of its intention
to terminate this Treaty, which renewed itself automatically. It
is therefore considered the longest "Treaty of Friendship" in modern
times, and has survived all the ebbs and tides of history.

Today, almost two centuries later, this Treaty of Friendship
still stands as a milestone in the history of this longstanding
relationship between Morocco and the United States, and illustrates
the deep-seated belief in friendship and freedom cherished by these
two peoples.

DOCUMENT 2 - 1840

AHMAD BIN NA'AMAN'S MISSION TO THE
UNITED STATES IN 1840
THE VOYAGE OF AL-SULTANAH
TO NEW YORK CITY

By Hermann Frederick Eilts

Source: Reprinted by the Embassy of Oman (Washington, D.C.) with
kind permission and corrections of the Author and the Essex Institute, Salem, Massachusetts, in whose Quarterly the article was
originally published in October, 1962.

Thursday, April 30, 1840, dawned slightly overcast in New York
City. Sometime after daybreak a bark hove to just off Sandy Hook,
where a revolving light marked the promontory of New York harbor,
there to take on a pilot. Under his helm, close-hauled before a
moderate southwest breeze, without the benefit of a steam tug, she
tacked slowly through the Narrows and into the bay beyond. Here
in the quarantine ground, she dropped anchor and waited to discharge
necessary port formalities. The bark was al-Sultanah (Sultani is
the common Arabic nautical colloquialism) 350 tons burden, eighty-
seven days out of Zanzibar.
     One figure stood out amongst this incongruous company. He
was a small, slighyly corpulent, bearded Arab gentleman, to whom
all paid deference. His complexion was tawny, his eyes were black
and piercing. Some were to describe him as fierce-looking; others
thought him handsome. A magnificent, gaily colored turban was on
his head. Around his waist was tied a cashmere shawl of equally
bright colors. Over a long white undergarment, he wore a beautiful
black robe, or gaftan, trimmed with gold and splendidly embroidered
at the shoulders. About his person hung an air of natural dignity.
     To the surprise of gaping port officials, he addressed them
in tolerable English. Quietly, but firmly, he announced that he,
not Sleeman, was in command (rais) of the vessel; his name, not that
of Sleeman, should appear on the port documents. It was done;
Sleeman's name was stricken. The arresting figure was Ahmad bin
Na'aman, special representative of Sayyid Said bin Sultan, Ruler
of Muscat, Zanzibar and their dependencies, in whose behalf he had
journeyed to the United States halfway round the world, on a mission
of good will and trade. Sultanah, the vessel which had brought him,
flew the unadorned, crimson ensign of his princely master and was the
pride of the Omani fleet. No sooner had she dropped anchor when a
boat from the 74 gun United States ship of the line North Carolina,
then in ordinary at the New York (Brooklyn) Navy Yard, drew along-
side. A trim, wide-eyed naval lieutenant boarded to tender the
services of his superior, Commodore James Renshaw, commanding the
Yard. The Commodore's courtesy was gratefully acknowledged. Two
days later, on May 2, with port formalities completed Sultanah tied
up to a wharf at the foot of Rector Street in the North River. The
first Arab emissary and the first Arab vessel to visit American shores
had arrived!

DOCUMENT 3

CORRESPONDENCE REGARDING THE TRIP OF
SUPERIOR GENERAL FATHER FLAVIANUS KFOURY
FROM KONCHARA, LEBANON, TO THE UNITED STATES
IN 1849

Source: "The Coming of the Arabic-Speaking People to the United
States", unpublished Ph.D. dissertation of Dr. Adele Younis, Boston
University, 1961.

Basilian Shoverite Order
Sup. General
Reg. III No. 478

St. John Convent, February 8th, 1961
Khonchara, Lebanon

Dir Sir:
    Answering to your letter dated 30/12/60 in which you call on us
to make a contribution concerning our late Superior General Flavianus
Kfoury who was the first man who came to the U.S. in 1849.
    After going over our records and documents, I found some impor-
tant records and informations which will help Miss Younis in her
subject.
    The reason for which our late Sup. General Flavianus Kfoury
traveled to the U.S. was to collect contributions in order to help
rebuild the Convent, because it was destroyed during the revolution
between the Christians and the Druzes.
    The above mentioned Father was recommended by his Archbishop
and many Bishops from the East and West. He spent in the U.S. about
two years or more, this is showed by the dated letters which we
keep in our records and the different recommendations given to him
in the U.S. from the Bishop of N.Y., Philadelphia, Rochester, Birmingham, Charleston and other Bishops. (See the Phot. records). So it
is showed by the permission given to him in Quebec from the Bishop
Peter Flavien TURGEON, Bishop of Sidyme in order to be allowed to
collect the contributions and exercise the Saint Mysteries according
to his particular Rite.

    Here is the translation of the French letter of Bishop Pierre
Flavien Turgeon:
    "We don't hesitate to permit to him (to Rev. Flavianus Kfoury)
to celebrate the Saint Mysteries according to his particular Rite (i.e.
Arabic Language) in all the Churches and Chapels of our Archdiocese.

Quebec 20th 1850
                "Pierre Flavien Turgeon
                Bishop of Sidyme"

    So I send here some photographed records in English Dated
1848 - 1850, with conformed copies in Latin and English Dated 1850 -
1851.

Please do understand that we are ready offer our services for the benefit of our Country.

Sincerely Yours,
Msgr. Augustin FARAH
Sup. General

Buffalo 28th July, 1850

Rt. LV Sir
The letters of this good priest from Syria are very satisfactory, but I am so poor, and my people are so poor that I can do no more then repeat what Bishop Hughes says on the opposite side of this sheet. I recommend this good priest to your kindness, he has permission to say mass.

+John Bp. of Buffalo

Wm O'Reilly
Rochester

To the Most Revd. the Archbishops and the Rt. Revd. Bishops of the Catholic Church in the United States -

The bearer of this the Priest Flavianus of the Monastary St. John Schweir in Mr. Libanus has brought us most excellent testimonials, and has been particularly recommended to us the Bishop of Beyrout and Mt. Libanus. He had commenced making a collection amongst the faithful of this Diocese but the coldness of the season and other circumstances has caused him to discontinue it until spring. In the meanwhile he has determined other parts of our country. We cheerfully and earnestly recommend him to the kind attention of the Hierarchy and Clergy of the United States.

+John Hughes
Bp. of N. York
By order of the Rt. Rev.
Bishop J.R. Bayley

DOCUMENT 4 - circa 1856

"SKETCH OF ANTONIA BISHALLANY
A SYRIAN OF MOUNT LEBANON"

By Rev. Charles Whitehead

Source: American Tract Society, 150 Nassau Street, New York
ca 1856

In October, 1854, Antonio landed at Boston, thankful to Him
who ruleth the winds and the waves, for the preservation of his kind
providence. The appearance of a city in this western world so different from oriental cities and towns in the style of architecture,
streets, conveyances, and costume of the people, must have deeply
interested him, and we presume that few objects escaped the notice
of his observing eye.

Having brought with him letters of introduction and recommen-
dation from the missionaries at Beirut to their Christian friends,
he at once sought them out, and was received by them with kindness
and courtesy.

DOCUMENT 5

A LETTER FROM ANDREW J. HUNT, A TEACHER
AT THE AMENIA SEMINARY, NEW YORK, TO
ANTONIO BISHALLANY, WINTER 1856

Source: "The Coming of the Arabic-Speaking People to the United States" by Dr. Adele Younis, Boston University, 1961.

We have many students this winter. All the rooms are full, but out of the whole company I have not found one who could declaim in Arabic. I hope you may return next term, for I think you would find Amenia very pleasant in the summer. I shall leave the school at the end of this term, but Mr. Foss will take my place, and he will take very good care of you. How do you stand this very cold winter? Do you have such snows on Mount Lebanon? I hope your health has not suffered from the severe frosts. Perhaps you are much better than if the winter had been more open. I will trust so at least.

By and by, Antonio, we shall reach a country better by far than either Lebanon or America. No bitter cold or burning heats there. I hope you are happy every day in prospect of that heavenly country, and happy, too, in the love of that dear Saviour, for whose sake you have left mother and native land. We do not forget to from for you when we meet in our prayerrooms, and hope that you do not forget me.

I am anxious to hear from you, and wish you would write me a letter, and tell all about your health and studies and prospects.

Remember I am used to your English, and can understand it pretty well. I shall hope to hear from you before many days.

I am your friend,
Andrew J. Hunt

DOCUMENT 6 - 1857-1866

"THE CAMELS THAT JEFFERSON DAVIS BOUGHT"

Source: The New York Times Book Review and Magazine, August 20, 1922

    Every man who ever had anything to do with the army is familiar
with the army camel, but not many of them know that Jefferson Davis,
when Secretary of War, commissioned a ship of the United States Navy
under Lieutenant, later Admiral, David Porter to go 5,000 miles for
its first real camels. Here is the documentary evidentce:

> Assistant Quartermaster's Office
> Indianola, Texas, February 10, 1857
> Sir: I have to report that 41 (forty-one)
> camels in good order were landed this day
> from the steamer Suwanee. I am, with
> respect, your obedient servant,
>   W.K. Van Bokkelan
>   Captain, Acting Quartermaster
> Hon. Jefferson Davis
> Secretary War, Washington

    What became of the camels? It is to be regretted that so pic-
turesque an experiment was not more successful. An official in the
office of the Adjutant General of the army, when inquiry was made
concerning the results of the venture...found time for a reply to
this effect: "It is shown by the records in the War Department that
after seven years trial it was demonstrated that camels were not
adapted for military transportation in this country. On March 18,
1866 the War Department authorized the quartermaster at New Orleans
to sell sixtv-six camels then in Texas, and those camels were sold
to the highest bidder, one Bethel Coopwood, San Antonio, Texas
at $31 a head."

DOCUMENT 7 - 1858

UNCLE SAM'S CAMELS

Source: The Report of Edward Fitzgerald Beale to the Secretary of
War Concerning the Wagon Road from Fort Defiance to the Colorado
River April 26, 1858, 35th Congress 1st Session House of Representatives
Ex. Doc. No. 124

Hon. John B. Floyd,
Secretary of War
June 25, 1857 - Left San Antonio at 1 P.M., and encamped at the
beautiful spring of the San Lucas, having made sixteen miles, the
camels carrying, each, including pack saddles, nearly five hundred
and seventy-six pounds. This being the first day, and the animals
not having performed any service for a long time, they seemed tired
on our arrival at camp; but I hope, as we proceed, and they harden
in flesh, to find them carrying their burdens more easily. Unfortunately, the only men in America who understand them, and who are
thoroughly acquainted with the mode of packing and journeying with
them, are some Turks, who came over with them, and who left at
San Antonio, refusing to go so long a journey, and alleging that
they had been badly treated by the government, not having received
the pay due them since January. It seems the appropriation having
been exhausted, no one is authorized to pay them, although they left
their own country under special contract with officers of the government and have performed their duties very faithfully. I have placed
the camels under the immediate charge of Mr. Breckenridge, Jr., assisted by Messrs. Morley and Via.
July 11...The camels are now keeping up easily with the train, and
came into camp with the wagons. My fears as to their feet giving
out, as I had been led to believe from those who seemed to know,
have so far proved entirely unfounded, though the character of the
road is exceedingly trying to brutes of any kind. My dogs cannot
travel at all upon it, and after going a short distance run to the
wagons and beg to be taken in. The camels, on the contrary, have
not evinced the slightest distress or soreness; and this is the
more remarkable, as mules or horses, in a very short time, get so
sorefooted that shoes are indispensable. The road is very hard and
firm, sharp, angular, flinty gravel -- very small, about the size
of a pea -- and the least friction causes it to rasp upon the opposing surface. The camel has no shuffle in his gait, but lifts
his feet perpendicularly from the ground, and replaces them, without
sliding, as a horse or other quadrupeds do. This, together with the
coarsely granulated and yielding nature of his foot, which though
very tough, like gutta percha, yields sufficiently without wearing
off, enables him to travel continuously in a country where no other
barefoot beast would last a week.

July 8. The more I see of them (the camels) the more interested
I become, and the more I am convinced of their usefulness. Their
perfect docility and patience under difficulties renders them in-
vlauable, and my only regret at present is that I have not double
the number.

DOCUMENT 8 - 1877

FIVE RECRUITED FOR TURKEY - STORY OF THE ARABS NOW AT
CASTLE GARDEN

Source: New York Daily Tribune, May 24, 1877, p. 7.

Seven Algerians, who claim to be escaped military prisoners
from French Guiana, arrived at the port a few days ago from Wilmington, North Carolina. Upon their arrival two of them went to Boston.
The others remain at Castle Garden. The mayor, having been informed
of their arrival, informed the steamship company that it would be
held responsible for any liabilities which these men contracted.
The company then offered to take them back to Wilmington, but they
refused to go for fear that the authorities there would send them
back to French Guiana, in which case they felt certain of being executed...

Their story as told to the reporter of the Tribune is as follows:
In January, 1876 during the French and Prussian War, the Algerians revolted. Ben Abed, then second in authority with his tribe
(and the others) were taken prisoner. The prisoners were then sent
to French Guiana where they remained about six years, working on
the roads. In May, 1876, fourteen of them made their escape in a
large government canoe. After drifting about for nearly two weeks,
they reached Domerara from where they wandered to Georgetown and
obtained emplowment. They staid there three months and saved about
125 francs, with which nine of them paid their passage to Trinidad.
They stopped there about six months working on the fortifications,
and them worked their passage to Wilmington, N.C. They remained at
Wilmington about six weeks tring to obtain work to unable them to
return to Tunis where their families reside, but they were arrested
as vagrants, and the Mayor to get rid of them paid their passage
to New York.

...Colonel H. S. Olcott, who interested himself last Fall in
behalf of nine Arabs who were in this country, called yesterday upon
those now at Castle Garden. The men are quiet and very attentive
to their religious duties. They go to the north-east side of the
building four times a day, and quietly perform their devotions, at
the same time "looking toward Mecca." They are all somewhat profici-
ent in the French language.

DOCUMENT 9 - 1881

SYRIANS IN AMERICA
EXPERIENCE OF THE FAMILY OF YUSIF ARBEELY

Source: New York Daily Tribune, June 20, 1881.

Yusif Arbeely, who with his wife and six sons came to this
country from Damascus, Syria, in August, 1878, arrived in this city
recently from Tennessee with his son Nageeb. The father is about
sixty years old and has many of the characteristics of his race.
He still adheres to the dress of his native country. He wore yesterday, a shirt made of purple silk striped with yellow, a fancy scarf
about his waist, baggy trousers buttoned at the ankle, and a red
cloth conically shaped hat, called a tarbush. Nageeb and his brothers
have only retained the red cloth cap. Both father and sons have
dark olive complexions, black eyes and black, crisp hair and beards.
Nageeb, who is very handcome, appears to be thirty, although he said
that he was only nineteen. The Arbeely family enjoys the distinction of being the only Syrian family that heas ever come to this
country to stay.

Yusif seems to take great satisfaction in relating his experiences since his arrival here and in giving his impressions of the
country. As he is not able to converse fluently in English, he is
compelled to speak through his son, who has acquired complete command on the language. After declaring his intentions to become
an American citizen, he said in conversation with a Tribune reporter
yesterday, that he took his family to Marysville, Tenn., on account
of its warm climate. Abraham, his eldest son, had since removed to
Austin, Texas, where he was practicing medicine; his second son,
Khaled, a druggist was also at Austin. All the other members of the
family were at Marysville. Fudlallah is a physician, Nageeb a student and teacher of French in the Marysville college, and the two
youngest, Habeeb and Nassiem, respectively fifteen and thirteen years
old, are in school. Respecting the last two, Yusif said he was
very anxious to secure them a collegiate education. Nageeb, in addition to his work in the college, frequently delivers lectures on
the members and customs of the people living in Syria.

"Yes," Arbeely continued, "the change from Damascus, almost
the oldest city in the world, to this the newest and most active
civilization in the world, was very great. But I have not been dis-
appointed. I left my relatives and friends behind because I desired
freedom of speech and action and educational advantages for my children. In coming here I have escaped the disadvantages of a retro-
grading civilization and a tryannical government, and have found
all that I came in search of. My friends were greatly surprised at
me. It was an experiment, but it has proved successful. You ask me
why more of my countrymen do not come. There are two things in the
way. One is that the Turkish Government is opposed to emigration
from the country not only discouraging it, but taking measures
against it; the other is that correct ideas of your great institutions here have not been spread among the people.

"I have been particularly pleased with the people here who are polite, agreeable in their manners, and have treated me with great kindness wherever we have gone. Your public schools and colleges have also made a strong impression upon me. The study of your political system has given me much amusement, particularly the struggle between the two parties for power. Democrats we? No, Republicans."

When asked if any of his sons had married yet he held up six fingers, and said that he hoped they would have the good fortune to find six good American young women for wives. Nageeb, smiling, nodded assent, and said that he and his older brothers had been taking lessons in courting, and were engaged in looking for wives now.

DOCUMENT 10 - 1885-1914

THE ROOTS OF SYRIAN ETHNICITY
THE BEGINNINGS OF A "SYRIAN - AMERICAN"
CONSCIOUSNESS

Source: The Syrian - Lebanese in America

By Philip and Joseph Kayal

A people organized socially around their religion and village express most of their values in relation to family life. It is the family that passes on the socio-religious values of the culture to its offspring. Indeed, proper introduction and identification of a Middle Easterner does not end with the announcement of his name and profession. Rather, his family group must be ascertained as well as his village community. For the Levantine immigrant, the family was an extension of himself, and his religion an extension of his family. For them, blood was not only thicker than water; it should never turn into water. The individual in isolation does not amount to much. He is complete as a social being only when related to his family and community. These are the primary units on whose foundation Middle Eastern culture has developed since biblical times...

The other important force in Syrian social life that affected the emergence of a strong community in the United States was religion. A Syrian's religious identification is so intense that he is the proverbial "man without a country." His patriotism and group identification is based on love for family and religion. For all practical purposes his family and church take the place of the state for him. In both Syria and Lebanon, religion is the practical equivalent of nationality, with each religious community recognized in and within the structure of the state. All cooperation between individuals, therefore, is limited to their traditional groups - family, village, and religion. This attitude was carried to America in the earliest stages of emigration and was an important factor not only in the structuring of the early Syrian - American communities but also in the present development (or lack of it) of Syrian ethnicity.

DOCUMENT 11 - 1891

"JEFF DAVIS' CAMELS IN ARIZONA"

By John L. Considine

Source: <u>Sunset</u> Magazine, May, 1923, p. 31

One morning in the latter part of October, 1891, bedlam broke
loose among the quadruped poplation of Harrisburg, Arizona. The
animals were headed pell-mell for the foothills one way when up the
street came the cause of the stampede, a bug bull camel which am-
bled into the corral enclosing the water supply.
"Leave him to me," said Harry Wharton as his puzzled townsmen
clustered about the corral gate. "I knew all about the brutes.
This is one of the bunch that Hi Jolly brought across the desert."

DOCUMENT 12 - 1896

THE "PREFACE" TO ENGLISH GRAMMAR (QUWAED AL-LOUGHA
AL-INGLEZEA) WRITTEN BY A.J. ARBEELY TO ASSIST
HIS NEWLY-ARRIVED COUNTRYMEN

Source: English Grammar by A.J. Arbeely, published in New York
City, 1896.

Many Arabic speaking people are constantly coming to this country and desire to learn the English language. In Egypt, Arabia and
all the oriental countries there is a rapidly growing desire on the
part of the people to learn this most widely spoken of all languages.
My desire to aid my own countrymen and others who seek to become acquainted with the language of this country, has led me to
prepare this textbook for the study of that language.
... (discussion of methodology).
At the request of many friends in this country therefore,
there has been added at the end of the grammar proper a key to the
work which will enable the English speaking student to learn Arabic
from this same book. At the end of the book will be found a long
list of the most important Arabic words arranged alphabetically and
defined.
I acknowledge with sincere gratitude my indebtedness to the
authors who have preceded me, whose valuable works have aided me in
the preparation of this work. Trusting my labor will not have been
in vain and that this work may meet the needs and receive the appro-
val of the friends who have been interested in its preparation, and
prove useful not only to my countryment and others who desire to
learn English, but also to students who are seeking a knowledge of the
the Arabic, I commend these pages to the kind favor of those whom
they are designed to aid.

A.J.A.
N.Y.C., Nov.15, 1896

DOCUMENT 13 - 1899

SYRIANS AND THE SULTAN
A Meeting at which a Revolution
in Turkey is Urged

Source: New York Daily Tribune, July 29, 1899, p.2.

An announcement appeared for several days in a number of Syrian papers printed in this city that Young Syria, a revolutionary society being organized in this city, would hold on Thursday night a mass meeting at Washington and Rector Sts. for the purpose of urging Syrians to write and to arm themselves against the Turkish Government. In view of this announcement the members of Young Syria and many other Syrians flocked to Washington and Rector Sts. on Thursday night, where they listened to speeches depicting the oppression of Syrians in Turley and denouncing the Sultan of Turkey. The speakers were four young men. They were deeply enthusiastic. They said the Turkish government should be overthrown... The speakers were frequently interruped by cheers, but there were many Syrians in the throng who ridiculed the utterances of the young men. "How far it is from New York to Constantinople!" exclaimed a man who was not in sympathy with the efforts of the speakers to incite a revolution.

DOCUMENT 14 - 1902

CASE HISTORY OF A FIRST-GENERATION IMMIGRANT IN DETROIT

Source: The Arab Moslems in the United States.

By Abdo Elkholy, College & University Press, New Haven.

Oue Detroit fellow came to America in 1902. His reasons for
leaving his country, Lebanon, or Syria as it was then called, were
political and economic. Syria at that time was, among many Middle
Eastern countries, a part of the Ottoman Empire whose satellites
suffered and bore heavy burdens of political submission, social in-
feriority to the Turkish ruling class, and economic obligations.
Everything was heavily taxed, even one's own garment; not more than
one member at a time of the large family could go outside or wald
in the street, for the garment had to be sealed to indicate the tax
payment.

The main reason for the emigration of our Detroit fellow was
the economic misery prevailing in his country. He was 25 years old
and mature enough to think of escaping his unhappy fate. He saved
a few liras which enabled him to buy his ticket to join some friends
on a boat to America in 1902. He did not know where he was going.
Knowing no English, he affiliated himself with some Syrian Christians
in New York City and followed their occupational pattern of peddling,
walking from one state to another. By the end of the year he found
himself in another Christian Syrian community in Detroit. He settled
down there ln 1903 as one of the city's few Moslems. In 1905, he
heard of some relatives who had come from Syria and immediately paid
them a visit, returning with a 15-year-old wife who during their
marriage bore him six children, three boys and three girls.

Our fellow made some money, enough to build his own home, but
not enough to go to the old country to show off. He still never
thought of establishing his life permanently in America. He bought
the house just to save the monthly rent, but was ready to sell it
any time he had made enough money to go back with his family. Having
been stupified by this dream of collecting enough money and going
back to the old country, he neglected to teach his children the instructions of his religion, for "very soon they would learn about
their religion back home in Syria," he said pitifully.

The years passed and he found himself engaged in the same kind
of job he had had when he first arrived: unskilled labor. One of
his two married sons was now divorced from his American wife who
claimed the children and brought them up as Christians; his three
daughters were married to American, Spanish, and Italian men. He
still did not know any more English for he lived in a rapidly growing Arab community. Since his children had married, he no longer
saw much of them. Many of his grandchildren married Americans and
drifted away from any religious ties they may have had.

Fifty-seven years in America did not change our Detroit fellow
much -- neither his outlook on life nor his dream of someday returning to the old country to settle there and end his journey. But
months after my interview with him, death ended his restless wandering.

DOCUMENT 15 - 1902

THE MELKITE RITE IN THE U.S.A.
THE INSTITUTUIONAL ACCOMODATION
OF A SOCIO-RELIGIOUS SUBSYSTEM

A discussion of the Melkite Church as it was
transplanted to the United States by its Arab parishoners

Source: Unpublished Masters Thesis by Rev. John A. Alya, Boston
College, Boston, Mass. 1962.

The Melkite Rite is one subdivision of the Eastern Catholic
rites. These latter are nowadays considered to be an essential part
of the Catholic Church, although they have definite particular status
different from that of the Latin majority. Sociologically speaking,
they can be considered as correlated subsystems under the great
socio-religious system which is the Catholic Church.
Imported sixty years ago, and transplanted outside its historical natural environment, the Melkite Rite in U.S.A. has been under-
going a wide range of accomodation. It has been facing many serious
problems which threaten its very survival...
The Melkites in fact form a very tiny minority inside the Catholic Church, namely less than .07% (seven for each 10,000 Catholics)
throughout the world, and a little more than .1% (1 for each 1,000
Catholics) in U.S.A. Their situation in the United States is still
more crucial than the foresaid proportion may imply. They are indeed
very dispersed all over the States...
The Boston parish, counts 1,620 members (441 families). This
is the most numerous Melkite parish in the United States after that
of Brooklyn, New York (about 700 families), and of Detroit, Michigan. According to a report presented in November, 1958 to the Archdiocese of Boston by Rt. Rev. Nicholas Borkhoche, B.S., then pastor
of Our Lady of the Annunciation Church, eighty-five Melkite "families" still lived at that time in the Central Boston area, at a
reasonable distance from the parish church. But forty of these were
formed of old aged persons living alone or in couples. Considerable
"clusters" of Melkites existed in West Roxbury and Roslindale, with
sixty-eight families in each one of these two localities. The next
locality was Quincy with fifty families. The following was Dorchester with twenty families. Eleven localities had two families each.
Thriteen localityies, (namely, Cohasset, Sharon, Melrose, E. Walpole,
Salem, Canton, Houghs, Neck Saugus, Situate, Hanover, Stoneham, E.
Boston and Readville) had one family each. Some of these localities
mentioned are about twenty miles from the church.
If Boston is next to the most numerous Melkite parish in the United States, it is not said, however, that it is the widest one. Saint
Ann's parish, in Los Angeles, California, is the only Melkite parish
in that state. It covers "as far as the pastor can reach!" Some
families registered in the parish are over seventy miles from their
parish church. This is oviously an extreme case. However, the fact

that the limits of the parish extend "as far as the pastor can reach"
is common to most of the Melkite parishes in America. Cities like
Boston, Brooklyn, Chicago, Detroit, Clevelnad, Los Angeles, and Milwaukee, with their vicinities or the entire State, have, respectively, one single parish.

DOCUMENT 16 - 1904

PENCIL AND WASH DRAWINGS BY GIBRAN KHALIL GIBRAN
A REVIEW

Source: Boston Evening Transcript, May 3, 1904, p.10.

Mr. Gibran is a young Syrian, who, in his drawings, manifests
the poetical and imaginative temperament of his race, and a remarkable rein of individual invention. The ponderous beauty and nobili-
ty of certain of his pictorial fancies are wonderful; and the tragic
import of other conceptions is dreadful. All told, his drawings make
a profound impression, and considering his age, the qualities shown
in them are extraordinary for originality and depth of symbolic significance. The series of drawings entitled "Toward God" (20), recently executed, is perhaps as remarkable as any of the works in the
exhibition. In spite of some crudity in the draughtsmanship, the
drawing called "Earth Takes Her Own" (20f), in this series, is fairly majestic in its meaning and expression. It reminds one of William Blakes's mystical works. Similar qualities are to be remarked in
"The Souls of Men" (11), "The Past: the Present: the Future" (925),
loaned by Mrs. J. Montgomery Sears, "Memory" (16), loaned by Mr.
Day, "The Lost Mind" (24), "The Dream of Life" (13), "The Descent
of Wisdom to India" (1), "One of the Worlds" (18), loaned by Miss
Josephine Preston Peabody, and "Light" and "Darkness" (22 and 23).
All these drawings are, as their titles imply, spiritual alle-
gories of the most solemn character and import. The earnest desire
to give expression to metaphysical ideas has triumphantly prevailed
over technical limitations to the extent that the imagination is
greatly stirred by the abstract or moral beauty of the thought.
There are faces here which haunt the memory with something of the
spell cast upon the fancy by the visions of dreamland; and, mingled
with some almost grotesque and repulsive types, incomplete reali-
zations of the artist's conceptions, wherein the hand has not been
able to answer to the idea, there is a whole gallery of gracious and
novel heads which express the purest aspirations and the most subtle
shades of moral moods.

DOCUMENT 17 - 1911

"SYRIANS IN THE UNITED STATES"
LOUISE HOUGHTON'S COMMENTS ON HER STUDY OF
THE SYRIAN PEDDLARS

Source: Survey, Volume 26, August 5, 1911, p. 647.

   ..."These peddlars refuse alms and resent any well-meant but
uncomprehending attempt to induce them to change their mode of life,
to give up peddling and go into a factory for example. The two
points of view are almost ludicously, if not tragically, apart.
They lie in different plains and are incapable of meeting. The
peddlar is a free man -- more often, no doubt, a free woman. Why
should she give up the open air, the broad sky, the song of the birds,
and the smile of the flowers, the right to work or to rest at her
own pleasure, to immure herself within four noisy walls and be subject to the strict regime of the clock? Why should she who has been
a whole person, become a mere "hand", and that the hand of another?
To one unfamiliar with the American industrial standard, the American
social viewpoint, the proposal is simply incomprehensible."

DOCUMENT 18 - 1925

MOSLEMS OF CITY CELEBRATING PIOUS FEAST OF RAMAZAN

RICH MERCHANTS FRATERNIZE THIS MONTH WITH
SWEATSHOP WORKERS AND BAKERS

Source: H.I. Katibah - <u>Brooklyn Eagle</u>, April 18, 1925.

Early Tuesday morning of last week a dingy "upper room" over the
Syrian cafe at 65 Washington St., hardly a stone's throw from the
towering giants of steel and mortar of the lower Manhattan District,
was filled to capacity by a motley crowd of pious Moslems of all
nationalities within the circumference of the Metropolitan area...

For it was the feast celebrating the passing of the fast month
of Ramazan, one of the three principal feast days on the Mohammedan
calendar...

Few Moslems there are who observe the rigorous fast of Ramazan
in the United States, which differs radically from our Christian
fasts in that it involves the complete abstinence from food, drink,
smoking or other earthly pleasures from early dawn to sunset. But
all share in the rejoicing of the feast alike.

Moslems in the U.S. about 30,000 in all represent all factions
and sects of Islam, Sunnites, Shiites, Nusairiahs, Druses, Matawilas,
Ahmadites and a few Sufi.

Almost half of their number make their home in Detroit working
in the Ford and other automobile factories.

New York Moslems have their own Imam, even if they do not have
a mosque. Perhaps this is due to the fact that there are very few
of them here, about 500 altogether.

DOCUMENT 19 - 1926

GIBRAN'S MESSAGE TO YOUNG AMERICANS
OF SYRIAN ORIGIN

By G.K. Gibran

Source: The Syrian World, July, 1926.

I believe in you, and I believe in your destiny.

I believe that you are contributors to this new civilization.

I believe that you have inherited from your forefathers
an ancient dream, a song, a prophecy, which you can proudly lay as
a gift of gratitude upon the lap of America.

I believe you can say to the founders of this great nation,
"Here I am, a youth, a young tree whose roots were plucked from
the hills of Lebanon, yet I am deeply rooted here, and I would be
fruitful."

And I believe that you can say to Abraham Lincoln, the blessed
"Jesus of Nazareth touched your lips when you spoke, and guided your
hand when you wrote; and I shall uphold all that you have said and
all that you have written."

I believe that you can say to Emerson and Whitman and James,
"In my veins runs the blood of the poets and wise men of old, and it
is my desire to come to you and receive, but I shall come with empty
hands."

I believe that even as your fathers came to this land to produce riches, you were born here to produce riches by intelligence,
by labor.

And I believe that it is in you to be good citizens.

And what is it to be a good citizen?

It is to acknowledge the other person's rights before asserting
your own, but always to be conscious of your own.

It is to be free in thought and deed, but it is also to know
that your freedom is subject to the other person's freedom.

It is to create the useful and the beautiful with your own hands,
and to admire what others have created in love and with faith.

It is to produce wealth by labor and only by labor, and to
spend less than you have produced that your children may not be de-
dendent on the state for support when you are no more.

It is to stand before the towers of New York, Washington, Chicago and San Francisco saying in your heart, "I am the descendant of
a people that builded Damascus, and Biblus, and Tyre and Sidon, and
Antioch, and now I am here to build with you, and with a will."

It is to be proud of being an American, but it is also to be
proud that your fathers and mothers came from a land upon which
God laid His gracious hand and raised His messengers.

Young Americans of Syrian origin, I believe in you.

DOCUMENT 20 - 1927

ECHOES OF THE SYRIAN REVOLUTION IN AMERICA

Source: Syrian World Magazine, February, 1927.

A fierce conflict is now raging among the Syrians in the United States which is the direct outgrowth of the war in Syria. Each party to the conflict is bombarding the other with the most virulent forms of accusations and invectives. So far, the batteries in action have been spouting only fire of a verbal nature, but there are hints of a fear of actual bloodshed. This possiblility, although remote from present indications, may yet lead to some regrettable incidents of physical encounter if passions that are now being fanned are allowed to run out of control. Lines of division among Syrian immigrants are being drawn sharper as actual hostilities in their mother-land show signs of abatement. And among Syrian immigrants who take part in home conflicts only from a distance and are not governed by feelings of an actual loss or a sense of genuine relief at the passing of a crisis, the effect of the controversy is more lasting, enmities are more enduring and the harmful results of dissensions are far more reaching.

What has given rise to this new outburst of feeling is the arrival in the United States of a delegation of the Syrian Nationalist party, headed by Emir Shekib Arslan, to attend the convention of the New Syria Party of America scheduled to open in Detroit, Michigan, on January 15th. Emir Shekib Arslan is a Druze and the personal representative in Europe of Sultan Pasha Atrash, leader of the Druze revolution is Syria. To counteract the possible accusation that the delegation, and consequently the cause that it represents, is partisan or religious, one Sunnite Mohammedan, Ihsan Bey Jabery, and two Christians, Nasim Bey Saybaha and Toufik Yazegi, were included in the personnel. Up to the time appointed for the opening of the convention only two members had arrived, namely: Emir Shekib Arslan and Nasim Bey Saybaha. No reason for the delay of the two others was given.

DOCUMENT 21 - 1928

"IN FAVOR OF TEACHING ARABIC"

The Teaching of Arabic to the Second Generation became a lively topic in The Syrian World magazine in 1928. Below are two
letters from the "Readers' Forum" column
of that magazine, published in New York
City, August 1928.

The debate now being conducted by The Syrian World on the subject
of the Arabic language should be of special interest to the Syrian -
American generation. We are now in a state of transition where we
need discussing such vital subjects to guide us along the proper
course and help formulate constructive opinions. And language being
the most potent factor in race solidarity, it is but proper that we
should give consideration to it first.

In my opinion, knowledge of Arabic would be a distinct asset to
the Syrian - American generation and all efforts to spread its knowledge should be commended. That it is not now generally taught is,
I must admit, the fault of the parents. I cannot shake off the con-
viction that most Syrian parents are woefully negligent in this respect. Some of them are even ashamed of their mother tongue and in-
different to their precious traditions.

In the same manner that we send our children to tutors for music, for instance, we can and should send them for learning Arabic.
It should also be the general rule that only Arabic be spoken at home.
The young generation may not appreciate all the benefits and advantages of knowing an extra language until later on in life, when it
would be too late to atone for the past.

We surely could make a better contribution to our beloved adopted country if we were better equipped linguistically, and consequently rendered more able to appreciate our racial heritage and pass it
along as our contribution to America.

                                        Clara K. Bishara.

    Brooklyn, N.Y.

September, 1928: "Neglect of Arabic Blamed on Parents"
The debate which is now being waged in The Syrian World about
teaching the younger Syrians in America the Arabic language, has
aroused our interests as much as it has the older people's...

In Lansing the young Syrian people, ranging from the ages of
sixteen to thirty, organized a club known as the "Young Phoenician
Society" whose purpose is to create a better understanding among the
young people.

Three months ago we decided to take twenty-five or thirty minutes from each club period which we held twice a month, and hold a
class for the purpose of learning Arabic. The teacher chose was a
very well-educated young man, and an instructor in one of the best
colleges in Michigan.

Everybody started out very enthusiastically for about four lessons, and after that nobody desired to advance any further. What was the trouble? It was that our parents didn't encourage us any further. They didn't have the patience to help their children, some wondered what good the Syrian language qould do them in America, and others didn't approve of it at all, and we ceased learning.

Therefore, I believe that the matter should be left to individuals to find means of teaching their children the Arabic language if they desire to, because it will be a tedious task to try to accomplish it universally.

Ruby Nakfoor
High School Student

Lansing, Michigan

DOCUMENT 22 - 1929

"EMIGRANTS VISIT HOMETOWN IN LEBANON"

By H.I. Katibah, Special Correspondent

Source: The Brooklyn Eagle, June 29, 1929.

Jdaidat Marj-Uyoun, Lebanon (By Mail) - This picturesque little town of Southern Lebanon may boast of its beautiful scenery and invigorating mountain climate, but it prides itself more particularly on two things -- at the fact that two-thirds of its population is now in America and that 100 percent of its children of school age are in schools...At a banquet attended by more than 20 persons, all men, there were at least six persons who had come recently form America to spend a summer in the old home town. Our host was a young man who hails from Flint, Michigan and who had come on the same ship with your correspondent. To my right was a young man from Brooklyn, and opposite me was another from Brazil. Not one of those I met who had come from America intend to live in Jdaidat; they all hanker to get back to the lands of liberty and plenty. Many of them have families in those countries and to their children the Jdaidat Marg-Uyoun is merely a jaw-breaker with vague images fantastically constructed from the reminiscent conversations of their parents.

...To the usual causes which keep the stream of emigration flowing from Syria there are two acute causes. These two causes are two revolutions in which the Jdaidites suffered heavily -- the revolution of 1919 and the recent one of 1925.

DOCUMENT 23

PHILIP HITTI'S COMMENTS AT TESTIMONIAL DINNER
FOR KAHLIL GIBRAN, JANUARY 5, 1929

Source: <u>Kahlil Gibran, His Life and World</u>, By Jean and Kahlil Gibran,
1974, p.391.

On January 5, 1929, Gibran was the recipient of tributes from
the Arabic - American colony. In honor of his twenty-five years
as a contributor to Arab letters, Arrabitah sponsored a testimonial
dinner at the Hotel McAlpin in New York. Among the eighteen speakers
was Philip K. Hitti, who summarized in English the pride that his
countrymen took in the man and his works.

The influence which Gibran exercises in modern Arabic literature can be measured, in a way, not only by the multitude of people
who have been benefited by reading him but also by the big crop of
would-be Gibrans, quasi-Gibrans and Gibran-imitators who have in
recent years, mushroom-like, sprung up and flourished all over the
Arabic speaking world. So much so that you can hardly nowadays
pick up an Arabic paper printed in Beirut, Cairo, Baghdad, Sao Paulo
or Buenos Aires without finding somebody consciously trying to write
Gibran-like. Of course, the esoteric, figurative, imaginative style
...is not a new thing in Arabic literature...But our hero of tonight,
through his unmatched mastery of this art, through his pure and rich
imagery, through his lofty and noble idealism, through his unexcelled
diction and compostition -- be it in Arabic, or in English -- has
become the father of a new school of thought all of his own. While
others use empty words, are affected and artificial, Gibran unfailing-
ly produces gems of thought and is always natural and sublime.

DOCUMENT 24 - 1929

SYRIAN FARMERS PIONEERS IN CALIFORNIA
"LETTERS TO THE EDITOR"- THE SYRIAN WORLD

Source: The Syrian World, January, 1929, p.50.

SYRIAN FARMERS PIONEERS IN CALIFORNIA
Editor, The Syrian World,
       In regard to the statement on Syrian farmers in the United
States I wish to add a little information to the survey already covered by Dr. Hitti in his book, "Syrians in America." An area in
central California was never touched by a plow owing to the fact
that it was a desert, and being such it was shunned by American
farmers and others until a Syrian from Zahle came along and bought
it from the State for a song. Immediately he and his son set to
work on this "desert" land and transformed it into one of the most
productive ranches in that district. The grapes he raised on it
captured first prize in an exhibition and the State sent a photogra-
pher to take pictures of the crops. Now our Bou-Najeeb owns several
cars and is living on Easy Street.

                                        Jamile J. Kanfoush

Syracuse, N.Y.

DOCUMENT 25 - 1930

THE "MAHRAJAN"(PICNIC) BRINGS THE DIVERSE
ARAB-AMERICANS TOGETHER

Source: "Hazardous Survival: Syrian-American Ethnicity", The
Syrian - Lebanese In America, by Philip and Joseph Kayal, Twayne
Publishers, Boston, pp. 193-194.

As an attempt at expressing and reaffirming the collective
sentiments of the Arabic - speaking communities in the United States
and encouraging in-marriage, the mahrajan was unsurpassed. Many small
and isolated communities sponsored the event each summer in a rotating
fashion which drew thousands of people from across the nation. At
first, it was used primarily for the in-group socializing and fund-
raising. In time, however, the composition and direction of the
mahrajan began to reflect the disposition and condition of the public
it was intended to serve. By 1960, the largest mahrajan in New England became settled in Danbury, Connecticut, and was sponsored by
the combined chuches and Syrian - Lebanese clubs of the city. Drawing more than 5,000 people every Labor Day weekend, the mahrajan
represents most clearly the melting of religious distinctions in
favor of a common and broader ethnic identity.

The avowed purpose of the event is to keep Oriental cultural
traditions alive among the young, and, by so doing, to achieve success in keeping them attached to their churches, which in turn means
attachment to their ethnic past. The emphasis is on culture -- food,
music, and dancing -- and not religious traditions per se, although
the churches are the principal forces behind the events. By helping
the young to identify themselves ethnically by placing before them
tangible evidence of their own history and culture, the Syrians expected that they will identify with one of the churches and hope-
fully seek a Syrian marriage partner.

In order that it be comprehensible and nonoffensive, the content
of the cultural heritage presented at these functions is highly limited and rather specific. In Danbury, it is generally acknowledged
that without the American and Americanized Arabic entertainment, it
would be very difficult to draw so many young people. And the young
do attend; over 60 percent of the attendance at these affairs consists
of single people below the age of thirty-five. While it seems that
most of the people there genuinely enjoy the Arabic entertainment,
it also appears that the young are more limited and very selective
about the type of Arabic music they respond to.

As a result, a new musical form, "Ameraba," has arisen which
while Eastern in inspiration, is essentially Western and often
played on Western instruments. It allows the listeners to participate actively by providing them with debke (circle dancing) music.
The debke is actually a Lebanese folk dance primarily intended for
weddings and has been refined and learned by all Arabic - speaking
Americans. While it originated in Mount Lebanon, it is presently
performed extensively by Syrians. However, the Syrians from Aleppo

.

and Damascus had to learn it from the "Lebanese" after they arrived in the United STates. The dance is hardly performed in modern Lebanon anymore and visitors from the Orient are amazed at its survival and the enthusiasm with which it is performed here. Undoubtedly, they miss the symbolic and emotional value of the dance.

DOCUMENT 26 - 1931

"SYRIANS OF BOSTON JOIN IMMIGRATION PROTEST"

Source: The Syrian World, January, 1931. Published in New York City, New York.

The proposal to halt immigration into the United States entirely for periods of from two to five years prompted leaders of various racial groups in Boston to hold a meeting of protest and communicate their disapproval to Congress.

Greeks, Italians, Jews and Syrians were represented at the meeting which was held on December 13 and reported by the Boston Herald of that date. The spokesman for the Syrians was Elias F. Shamon, an attorney and president of the Massachusetts Syrian Association of American Citizens. The Boston paper reported him as having summed up the objections to the proposed complete ban on immigration as follows:

Only 123 Syrians are permitted to enter the United States yearly, and to pass the proposed measure would do a great injustice to a land which has been sorely neglected by the co-called ethnologists set up by Congress to determine the nationality of people in this country under the national origin act.

The present protective law is sufficient, and to pass an act of complete annihilation of immigration will be interpreted by the world not as a protective measure, not as an aid in the interests of ameliorating economic conditions, but rather will be viewed, and rightly so, in the light of the vindictive and acrimonious proponent of the national origin act, as more fuel added to the fire which preceded the welding of that act.

DOCUMENT 27 - 1931

"HEALTH PROBLEMS OF SYRIANS IN THE U.S."

By F.I. Shatara M.D., F.A.C.S.

Source: The Syrian World, March 1931, New York, New York.

"A brief mention should be made of tuberculosis and other lung
infections such as pneumonia, pleurisy, ets. While no statistics
are available, I am under the impression that the Syrian is more
prone to these diseases than the native-born. The reasons for this
are several. The climate in Syria is mild and equable, while here
it is severe and changeable. There is sometimes, as is commonly
known, as much as forty degrees variation in temperature within
twenty-four hours. Again the change from an out-of-door life to
a life of confinement where one rarely sees the sun, and inhales
instead of pure air, one that is laden with smoke and dust, breaks
down the resistance and renders one susceptible to these lung diseases. The Syrian working girl is the one especially to suffer.
She divides her life between the tenement house, the factory and
the subway, gets very little exercise and recreation, and after
living about two years in a city like New York, loses her vitality
and healthy color, and becomes an easy prey for these diseases.

In conclusion, I must briefly and cautiously mention venereal
diseases. It is a difficult matter to discuss these days without
committing a breach of propriety. On the other hand the prevalence
of these diseases, which are often contracted because of sheer ig-
norance, leads me to believe than an educational campaign along
these subjects is a greatly needed one, and one that will save our
Syrian youth many sufferings and dire consequences. Let the family
physician assume the role of teacher and guide. Let parents realize
that knowledge properly imparted, far from hurting the morals of
children, will dispel that morbid curiosity which often leads youth
astray.

DOCUMENT 28 - 1936

"BOYS MASTER THE KORAN IN ARABIC"

Source: Cedar Rapids Gazette, January 12, 1936.

Two Cedar Rapids' boys have mastered the reading of the Koran
or Moslem bible in the Arabic language and delighted a congregation
with their first public readings last Sunday in the local Moslem
Temple at 1335 Ninth St. N.W.

The youths, both American born, are Abdallah Igram, 12, son of
Mr. and Mrs. Hassan Igram of 511 M Avenue N.W., and Hussen Sheronick,
7, son of Mr. and Mrs. Aleck Sheronick of 1436 L Street S.W., Abdallah, born in Cedar Rapids, is a 6-A student at Harrison School and
a talented cornetist. Hussen is a pupil at Van Buren School.

The two boys are said to be the first in the U.S. to achieve
a reading knowledge of the Koran in a temple class, practically all
study of this type having been heretofore conducted privately.

DOCUMENT 29 - 1937

HE LEARNED TO READ FROM COMIC STRIPS:
Faris Malouf, City's New Street Commissioner,
Came to America 30 Years Ago

By Louis M. Lyons

Source: <u>Boston Sunday Globe</u>, April 4, 1937.

The streets of Boston which will come under the care of Faris S.
Malouf as the city's new street commissioner look very different
to him than the first roads he trod in America.

Those were hot, weary, dusty farm roads of Georgia. A 15-year
old immigrant boy who knew two words of English trudged 15 to 20
miles a day with a 20-pound pack on his back, peddling dry goods and
notions from door to door. He had his prices marked in Arabic on
his goods. He made his sales by showing his wares and by the eloquent
use of his hands and his great brown eyes.

That was 30 years ago. The speecnless peddler of 1906, now a
successful member of the bar, became last week the first of the Lebanese and Syrian people to win a place in the City Government of Boston.

Next to Angels

Faris Malouf's 30 years in America epitomizes a phase of life in
this land that makes this country wear a different look to Old World
peoples than any other land on earth. His American career is one
leaf from the lives of the 10,000 of his fellow countrymen of the
mountain of Lebanon and of the surrounding Syrian plain who have become citizens of Boston within a single geration. It is a glimpse
of the experience of millions more first generation Americans.

Faris Malouf had been two days in America when he had his first
lesson in Americanization. It was a hard one but it lasted. He and
a brother, a year older, landed in New York with $4 between them.
Countrymen put them up and saw them on their way to Atlanta, where
they had distant cousins who had started a few years before as ped-
dlers and become small merchants.

"We thought Americans were next to angels, "Malouf laughs as
he tells his story. "The only Americans we knew were American missionaries at the University of Beirut. From them we judged that this
was a land of perfection. It was every youth's ambition to come to
America."

That illusion didn't last.

Victims of Fakir

They got through Ellis Island on a Friday. On Sunday the two
wide-eyed Byzantine lads were standing in front of the house of their
countryman when two men offered them two valuable rings for the incred-
ible price of $1.50. It seemed a great stroke of fortune. But this

was America and here was opportunity. Withing a few minutes the lads
rushed in upon their hospitable friend to show their jewels. He
gave a bitter laugh and told the boys the rings weren't worth a dime.

But the Georgian farmers were kind to the boy peddler. Often he
slept in their homes, though many of his wayside customers had no
beds even for themselves. Malouf had to reform his picture of America in the face of the poverty of the Southern small farmer and the
treatment of the Negro. But he made money peddling, often $4 or $5
a day, which he sent home to his father. Even prouder than of the
money was the boy of his progress in the language. One quest he re-
calls in those first months. He asked for two days until he found
a house with an atlas, and from it he copied out "Beirut" in English
and addressed a letter to his father, explaining inside that he had
written the address in English himself.

Came to Boston

His older brother did not live to become established in the new
land. Faris Malouf's own health could not stand the trudging pack-
laden days. After a year and a half of peddling, he returned to
New York. But he found nothing there and came on to Boston. He had
no money and all he could find for a year was a job cleaning the
glass in a glass factory in South Boston at $7 a week. His room cost
him $2.25 a month. At the end of a year he looked for a better job
and found it as an edge setter in a shoe factory. He was earning a
little more and after a year in Boston he married, when he was still
under 18, a girl who had been a neighbor in Lebanon.

He stayed nine years in the shoe factory. The first year after
he married he went to an evening class to learn the English alphabet.
They taught him "This is my hand" and "This is my foot." It helped
him in speaking the necessary work-a-day language of the shop. But
he did not learn to read or write.

The impulse to get an education in English came to him out of
one of the great tragic stories of modern times. One day when he
pushed into the subway turnstile the newpapers that people were reading looked strangely exciting and everyone was excitedly reading.
He bought a paper. It told him nothing. So he bought another and
still learned nothing. "What is it?" he asked a fellow straphanger.
"Can't you read?" returned the other. "No," Malouf acknowledged.
The other said something about "Titanic," but Malouf's station was
reached just then and he went to the shop still ignorant. A friend-
ly man named Patrick Kenndey at the next bench in the finishing room
told him the story of the sinking of the Titanic.

Learned to Read from Comics

"I bought a newpaper every morning and every evening from that
day," says Malouf. "Uncle Dudley was a great part of my education.
But I learned to read from the comic strips. It was easy English
and I mastered all the comic strips first. From that I went on to
other parts of the paper. After that beginning my Arabic Bible taught
me English faster than anything elase. I would prop it up on the
window sill of the factory, with an English Bible beside it. The

verses are numbered the same and both in Arabic numerals. So I would
match the verses. When I found a hard word Patrick Kennedy would
help me on it."

From his Bible lessons he got enough English to begin evening
school work with the fifth grade and to complete the course at the
Franklin Grammar School on Waltham St. in April, 1920. Malouf was
28 and his younger classmates chose him to deliver their graduation
oration. He built his address upon an Arabic verse that runs:
If there be a day in which I gain no knowledge
That day shall never, never be counted in my days.

Impressed His Teachers

His teachers were impressed with the style and thought of Malouf's compositions. They urged him on to higher education. He had
by now put his shoe factory days behind him. He had worked in the
shipyards in 1917. He had become the president of the Syrian Club
of Boston and led in Liberty Loan drives and other war-time work
among his people.

A younger brother who had joined him and had lived at his house
came back from the army to marry and start a small manufacturing
business. The two brothers and their wives shared the same home.

Faris Malouf became part owner and manager of a bakery to serve
the special Syrian clientele with the hard-baked loaves of their native dietary. The bakery was a successful venture. He sold out his
interest after 10 years to become superintendent in the developing
curtain-manufacturing enterprise of his brother and sister-in-law.

Their business experience was a swift spelling of the opportunity that so many of their alert race have found in America. Starting only a dozen years ago with a few hundred dollars, their art
curtain business has become a $250.000 industry. Faris Malouf left
their business to enter the law.

Ambition for Law

He had gone on with his studies, first in evening high school
then at Northeastern University evening courses. But he had already
become a leader among his people at 30 and he found an increasing
desire to make his career in the law.

This ambition goes back to his boyhood in a village of Lebanon.
The Lebanese, descendants of the ancient Phoenicians, have remained
the proud heirs of a cultural and commercial leadership of Asia
Minor. Malouf's own grandfather was British consul at Beirut, a man
of learning who lectured at the Asiatic Club in London, became in-
terpreter to Lord Raglan, commander of the British forces in the
Crimean War, and received honors at the hand of his Suzerain, the
Sultan of Turkey.

The father of Faris Malouf was a doctor in their village, and
the man of learning among the unlettered people of the surrounding
farmers. They came to him with the problems raised by official and
legal requirements. The doctor wrote out their papers and petitions.
Faris Malouf remembers how it was the talk of the village that the
doctor one day wrote 45 letters in two hours. Faris as a boy used

to bask in the prestige that his father enjoyed for his learning.
He used to write out letters in the pointed Arabic script, and dream
of a time when he would be such a scribe to the people as his father.
The land was poor, for all his rich spiritual heritage as the
cradle of the three great religions - Hebrew, Mahometan and Christian.
Immigration had just got underway when Faris Malouf was born in 1892.
All the villagers had kinsmen in the Americas sending home letters
and money by the time he was a lad at the priest's school.

Immigrant

The Lebanese flowed across the sea, to South as well as North
America. His own father left, as so many of the family heads did, one
year, and took his oldest son to Brazil, where he established him in
an import trade that has grown to this day. But Dr. Malouf did not
sent for his wife and younger children to join him in the new land,
as was the ususal case with the Syrian immigrants. The doctor returned to his homeland. When Francis was 15 it took months of plead-
ing for him and his brother to get their father to let them leave
for America. It was their mother who finally joined her pleas to
theirs. After all, they could always return.
Until he was deep in his 30's Faris Malouf always had a consciousness that he had not risen in the new land to the level of his
family background in old Lebanon. As he became a man of substance
and with education, his people came to him often with their papers
and problems, as they had to his father in the old land. But he
was not a lawyer and he saw the disabilities his peoples had before
the law because not only their language but their ways of thought
were so alien to Anglo-Saxon thought.

Law School

When he was 32 he applied to enter law school. The Northeastern law dean found him shy two points of entrance requirements. Malouf persuaded him by much arguing that he had an equivalent education in Arabic which should count. As a concession the dean sent
him to Prof. Jewett at Harvard for an examination in Arabic. On
that examination he was admitted to law school.
He studied enormously. From his first attendance at evening
grammar school until his graduation at law school, he never missed
a session. He was superintending the curtain manufacturing, leading
his Syrian community activities, taking a leading part in the Boyls-
ton Congregational Church, where he is now deacon and chairman of
the prudential committee and carrying a full law course.
His final burst of studying almost undid his career. He gave
up his business in April, 1928, to devote a full 12-hour day to pre-
paring for his bar examinations in June. As the time approached he
stretched the 12 hours to 16 hours. Four days before the examination
date he fell exhausted over his table in the Y.M.C.A. reading room.
Not daring to go home for fear his wife would put him to bed and
end his frenzied preparation, he hired a room, slept four hours and
went on studying till midnight.

He had learned a great deal, but not how to study. He came to
his examination with a mind that he describes as "blank". He knew
he had failed. But that did not take the chilling edge of dismay
off the notification of failure when it came in August.

Like a Dead Man

"I had never failed at anything in my life" he says. "I felt
like a dead man. For days I was numb. Everything was lost. My
whole life plan was broken up. But after a while I suddenly snapped
out. My courage came back. I spent the next few months taking a
special preparation for the bar examination. In December I took it
again and I knew that time that I could win no matter what they asked
me."

At 36, Malouf began his law career. He had become a citizen in
1915. His leadership among the Lebanese and Syrians of the city was
greatly enhanced now that he was an attorney with an office at 73
Tremont St. His people had few spokesmen at the bar. His position
in his community reached a peak when he was chosen president of the
Syrian and Lebanese American Federation of the Eastern states, an
organization he helped to found in Boston in 1932. He is now serving his second term as its president. Its purpose, stated in the
Constitution he helped to frame, includes a "real adherence to good
Government and uncompromising abhorrence of all forms of political
corruption."

Friend of Mansfield

Malouf heard Frederick Mansfield speak on Boston Common in 1929.
He was impressed. When later he needed a lawyer of larger experience in an important long-drawn out case, he secured Mr. Mansfield.
Out of tht association came Malouf's adherence to Mr. Mansfield in
the campaign of 1933 that saw the Syrian community support him almost
unanimously.

"I take Mayor Mansfield's appointment as recognition of our
people rather than of me personally," says Faris Malouf of his appointment to the Board of Street Commissioners. "I count it my duty to
justify that confidence and serve as a credit to the citizens of
Syrian and Lebanese extraction. I feel strongly that our people with
their ancient heritage as a source of religious and of civilization
have something of value to contribute to the city and state, and
that they should be given an opportunity to make their contribution."

DOCUMENT 30 - 1939

"A SHEIK GROWS IN BROOKLYN"

By William Peter Blatty

Source: <u>Which way to Mecca Jack?</u>, Published by Bernard Geiss Associates, New York, 1957.

...in the summer of 1939, the President himself visited our neighborhood to officiate at the formal opening of the Queens Midtown Tunnel. The tunnel spilled out onto East 35th Street, just three doors down from our apartment building, and "I wanna meet him," rumbled Mama when she heard FDR was coming. My uncles -- Moses, Elias, and Abdullah -- told her it was "impossible."

On the day of the ceremony, my mother and I, together with my uncles, were standing at the outer circumference of a cordon of spectators about thirty feet from the President's automobile. In her left hand, Mama held a mysterious, brown paper shopping bag, but I paid no attention to it at the time.

All eyes were on FDR as he reached out from his car with a gold-plated scissors and neatly snipped the broad, blue ribbon that stretched from one side of the tunnel entrance to the other. Then, before anyone knew what was happening, my mother was grimly advancing on the President. It must have looked like an assiassination attempt, because flasbulbs started exploding,the President dropped the scissors in horror, and a covey of Secret Service men drew their revolvers and surrounded the car.

They were too late. Mama had gotten to the President.

"I wanna shake you hand," she rumbled at FDR, and then she reached out and crunched the President's paw in her effortlessly dynamic grip. FDR smiled weakly.

When Mama leaned over and reached into the mysterious shopping big, two of the Secret Service men made a dive for her, but they barely got a glove on my mother before she had withdrawn from the bag a large jar filled with a murky, rust-colored substance. She handed it to the astonished President.

"Homemade jelly," Mama grunted. "For when you have company."

"Might be nitro, Chief!" warned one of the Secret Service men. But FDR winked at him and accepted the jar. "Thank you, Madam," he said.

"Quince jelly," added my mother matter-of-factly. "Lebanese quince jelly. My God, it's delicious!"

FDR smiled and shook my mother's hand again, and I had to card him for sheer guts.

Three Secret Service agents escorted Mama back to the spectator's circle, and as her gaze fell upon my uncles her eyes flickered briefly with triumph. She was unstoppable and she knew it.

DOCUMENT 31 - 1941

A LETTER FROM FRANKLIN DELANO ROOSEVELT

THE WHITE HOUSE
WASHINGTON

July 12, 1937

TO THE MEMBERS OF THE SYRIAN-AMERICAN SOCIETY OF SOUTH CAROLINA:

Syria has stood throughout the ages at the conjunction of mighty events in world history. Men of Syrian blood who have come to the United States have brought with them rich memories of an ancient heritage.
    We have welcomed them to our shores and in their new homes they have made a distinct contribution to our social, political and economic life. It gives me, therefore, great pleasure to send the members of the Syrian-America Society of South Carolina my hearty felicitations and warm wishes that their convention at Columbia will be fruitful of happy results.

Franklin D. Roosevelt

DOCUMENT 32 - 1941

"MEMORY OF KAHLIL GIBRAN RECALLED BY EXHIBITION"

By A.J. Philpott

Source: <u>Boston Daily Globe</u>, December 10, 1946.

When an artist is dead 15 years he is usually forgotten -- except by a few friends. Occasionally one survives because of his
work and character. Among the later it might be well to mention at
this time Kahlil Gibran, painter, sculptor, poet and philosopher,
who died in New York in 1931. He was world-famous when he died.

As a boy he lived in the Syrian colony on Tyler St., Boston,
and graduated from the old Quincy Grammar School on Way St., in the
South End. He then went to college in Beyreuth, Syria, after which
he studied in the Sorbonne. in Paris. He came back to Boston and studied art here for a few years. He then went to Paris where he studied
painting with some of the best artists, and sculpture under the famous Rodin.said of Gibran: "He is the William Blake of the 20th century, and one of the few living men who has a true sense of form."

Although he was famous as an artist, Gibran's greatest fame
came to him as a writer, His books have been translated into 14 languages. He was a great Arabic scholar, and many of his books were
first written in Arabic. He was very popular in all of the Arab
countries, including Egypt.

There was something of the spirit of Omar Khayam in Gibran, also something of the spirit of Confucius -- except that he was more
spiritual than either, and more mystical. There is something of the
sonorous and musical quality of the Psalms in most of his writings,
especially in "The Prophet," "The Madman" and "Jesus, the Son of Man."

He had a host of admirers in France, England and the United
States. Chief among these in America were Amy Lowell and Theodore
Roosevelt's sister, Mrs. Robinson. In fact, his writings were gener-
ally admired by the literary elite of his time.

After his death in New York the body was brought to Boston and
a funeral service held in the Syrian Maronite Catholic Church on Tyler St., "Lady of the Cedars." It was then placed in a vault in Mt.
Benedict Cemetery for three months until arrangements had been made
for its removal to Mt. Lebanon, where it was buried in the little
town of Bsherri where Gibran was born, close to the famous Cedars
of Lebanon. His sister accompanied the body from Boston to its final
resting palce with Gibran's ancestors. The Lebanese have built a
museum in Bsherri, which contains many of Gibran's paintings, drawings, and sculptures, and many of his original manuscripts.

His memory is recalled by reason of the fact that there is now
an exhibition of some of Gibran's art works in Knoedler's art gallery
in New York. In reality, Gibran was a Boston artist -- one of the
forgotten. But he was too great to remain in oblivion.

DOCUMENT 33 - 1950

"PURPOSES AND POLICIES OF THE
SYRIAN AND LEBANESE AMERICAN FEDERATION
OF THE EASTERN STATES"

By James M. Ansara, Executive Secretary

Source: The Federation Herald .

The purposes and policies of the Syrian and Lebanese American
Federation of the Eastern States, after almost a quarter of a century of existence, should have become matters of public record. Year
after year they have been clearly and consistently demostrated in
the Federation's activities -- in its annual conventions and conferences, its publications, its lectures, forums and panel discussions,
its varied educational programs, and in its numerous public statements and reports.
    The basis of the Federation and its underlying purposes are
clearly enunciated in its Constitution's preamble and Article I,
ehich read:
    "We, American citizens of Syrian, Lebanese and other Arabic-
speaking stock or extraction, being deeply conscious of our common
ethnic heritage and our close blood and cultural ties, and being
desirous of uniting our efforts and resources for the purposes hereinafter set forth, and acting through representatives of local organizations, do hereby create the Syrian and Lebanese American Federation of the Eastern States and establish this as our Constitution."
    "The purpose of the Federation shall be to promote by precept
and example the highest ideals and aims of American citizership, and
shall assist in the formation of an enlightened public opinion as a
guide to our government, public institutions general public in their
efforts to promote a better understanding and more peaceful relations
among the nations of the world, to the end that the dignity, freedom
and security of mankind may be strengthened and firmly eatablished.
In this éndeavor, the Federation shall give special attention to the
relations between the peoples of the United States of America and
those of the Arabic-speaking world."

DOCUMENT 34

THE ISLAMIC FEDERATION, 1952:
"Muslims in the American Mid-West"

By Umhau Wolf

Source: The Muslim World, Volume L, January 1960, pp. 42 and 43.

The Federation of Islamic Associations is the official organization in the United States and Canada. It is the nearest thing to
a synod although it is primarily concerned with Muslim society and
not narrow to "church affairs". It developed out of the dreams and
torments of a young Muslim soldier in the United States armed forces
in World War II. He had difficulty with the "dog-tag", since he did
not wish to be a Protestant (the usual government term for anything
non-Catholic). But just as surely he was not a "blank", with no
religion. When Ab-dallah Igram from Cedar Rapids, Iowa, was dis-
charged in 1945 he kept working on his problem and a dream. He became the father of five children and in 1958 was named "Outstanding
Young Man of the Year" by the Cedar Rapids Junior Chamber of Commerce.
In 1952 the Cedar Rapids Muslim community issued an open ivitation
to Muslims for a convention to be held there. It was an appropri-
ate place since in 1933 the first Muslim mosque in the Western Hemisphere had been erected in Cedar Rapids, although it was not the
first building used as a mosque. More than four hundred Muslims
responded and on June 28, 1952, the International Muslim Society
was created. Naturally, Mr. Igram was elected president and served
for three years.

The second convention was held in 1953 in Toledo, Ohio. More
than one thousand persons from the United States and Canada attended the various sessions. A committee to draft a constitution was
appointed. Because of the enthusiasm engendered and the cohesion
gained, the Toledo community began a drive for a new mosque which
was dedicated in 1954. The Chicago convention of 1954 saw the re-
alization of a strong organization with the adoption of a constitution and the statement of the broad purpose of the organization.
On July 10, the new name, "Federation of Islamic Associations in
the United States and Canada" was officially adopted. Previously,
the entire assembly elected officers and they bore the full responsibility. Now a Board of Directors was added which gave proportion-
ate representation to individual societies so that local groups
would feel a part of the program and promote its purposes. Mr. Igram
would not run again, ard so in London, Ontario, Colonel Hassen Abraham, of South Bend, was elected president in 1955. He presided over
the next two conventions which were exceptionally large: New York,
1956 and Detroit, 1957. During these years the convention was the
responsibility of the host community. At the Detroit convention
in 1957, Mr. Qasim Olwan was elected third president. He had been
treasurer from its inception. With this meeting the Federation as-
sumed responsibility for its conventions in cooperation with the
local societies. From this time on, the Board of Directors' meetings
have been opened to any who wish to listen or to speak.

DOCUMENT 35 - 1952

PREAMBLE TO THE
CONSTITUTION OF THE FEDERATION OF ISLAMIC ASSOCIATIONS
IN THE UNITED STATES AND CANADA

Source: The Islamic Center, Washington, D.C.

PROCLAMATION

We, the members of the Moslem Community of America, following
the Koramic injunction, "Hold fast, all of you Moslems, to the rope
of God and do not disperse," resolve to combine our endeavor the
purposes hereinafter set forth do hereby proclaim the formation of
the Federation of Islamic Association in the United States and Canada.

PREAMBLE
Every human being according to Islam is born pure by (fitrah)
and bears within himself a Trust to know God and worship Him. In
the pursuit of this ultimate end, the foremost obligations of the
Moslem in this world are the acquisition of Knowledge and Experience.
His guides in this inescapable endeavor are the Quran and the Sunnah
revealed as an act of Mercy to assist man in the fulfillment of his
Ends. A devoted Moslem constantly strives through the careful nur-
turing of his soul and his body, to transform his whole personality
and his attitudes to higher and higher levels of being, whereby his
spiritual, moral, intellectual, and social ideals of mankind.
Moslems, wherever they are and in whatever age they live are
individually and collectively responsible to learn, exercise and
spread the ideals of Islam, such as the dignity and supreme worth
fo every human being, brotherhood, and love among all mankind, and
the absolute equality of every person before God. Their mere pro-
fessing of the principles of Islam is the lowest degree of being a
good Moslem.
As an expression of their obligations and services in the path
of God, the Moslems of the United States and Canada shall organize
themselves under the present constitution to promote and teach the
spirit, ethics, philosophy, and culture of Islam among themselves
and their children. They shall through this organization establish
close contacts with all parts of the Moslem world and participate in
the modern renaissance of Islam.
They shall try, through publications and otherwise, to expound
the teaching of Islam and clarify its ideals and spirit. In this
endeavor they shall try to point out the common grounds, beliefs,
and common ends which other religions share with Islam.
In this age of international strife and unrest, they should
draw on the spiritual, moral, and intellectual wealth of the Moslem
civilization and contribute their proper share in the establishment
of world peace.
The Moslem communities in the United States and Canada should
organize themselves into Local Associations to translate the above

objectives within their communities. These local organizations should, besides the teaching and observance of the principles of Islam, adminsister to the religious needs of the members of their community. They should also provide media for the religious, intellectual, and social needs of their members, and tender them with moral, legal, and finanacial comfort.

DOCUMENT 36 - 1953

MESSAGE FROM THE WHITE HOUSE

The White House
Washington   July 13, 1953

    I am happy to extend my greetings to the National Association
of Federations of Syrian and Lebanese American Clubs and to all its
regional Federations.

    As Americans of Syrian and Lebanese ancestry you have done much
to bring about closer understanding between the peoples of the United
States and the Near East. And as loyal American citizens you have
won renewed regard and respect for the ancient and majestic heritage
you represent.

Dwight D. Eisenhower

DOCUMENT 37

THE TOLEDO MOSQUE, 1953
"MUSLIMS IN AMERICAN MID-WEST"

Source: THE MUSLIM WORLD, Volume L, January 1960, p.44.

The Toledo mosque was made possible by the stimualtion from
the Federation convention in 1953. Located just off one of the busy,
through-streets in town, it is in an old neighborhood just about a
mile from downtown. Its members come from all over the district.
They have frequent social events to which non-Muslims are invited,
as well as certain cultural interchanges. The mosque, which cost
about $100,000 is now free of debt. It is a true mosque, with up-
stairs for religious purposes only, and downstairs for social and
business activities. There were no pledges but various men's, women's and youth organizations raised the funds by dues, suppers,
bazaars, dances, etc. It is legally incorporated by the laws of
Ohio as a religious society. Its officers are volunteers who serve
as a Board of Trustees. There are about six or seven lay preachers
who give the sermon now in the absence of a full-time imam. When
Mr. Avdich was present, the Friday sermon was given in both Arabic
and English. Now it is only in English. Arabic classes are held
for children. The Sunday School is conducted at 11 A.M. and during
the winter months averages 150 persons from four years to adult.
Three lay teachers are in the elementary department. Mr. Avdich
recently published a text for use with young people and adults,
which is being adapted by teachers of small children. The second
great need of American Muslims is for educational materials. There
is no library in this mosque. The imam's personal library was used
when he was abailable. The mosque is open all day for prayer. The
Toledo mosque has the only resident paid custodian in an American
mosque. The leaders are highly respected members of Toledo society
and their greatest desire is to find a full-time imam as soon as
possible.

DOCUMENT 38 - 1955

"SUNDAY SCHOOL IN TOLEDO"

Source: The Arab Moslems in the United States, by Abdo A. Elkholy,
College & University Press, New Haven, Connecticut 1966, pp. 133-135.

Sunday is not the only active day in the Toledo mosque. There
are many activities every day: at least one religious group comes
daily from different religious faiths and institutions to acquaint
themselves with their Moslem fellow citizens; there are occasional
meetings and parties; at certain times one is always sure to meet
the religious leader of the community in the mosque. Nevertheless,
Sunday is the most active day of the week in the regular life of
the mosque. It is the day of Sunday school and practically every
family brings its children to the school to learn about their religion. There are about 150 students enlisted in the school, ranging
in age from 4 to over 15. The five classes, along with their distribution according to age, are presented in Table 58.

Table 58
SUNDAY SCHOOL IN TOLEDO, BY GRADES AND AGE DISTRIBUTION

Grade	Age	Number	Curricula
1	15+	80	Islamic history and philosophy
2	10-14	15	Religious practices with their social significance
3	7-9	15	Basic Islamic pillars and beliefs
4	4-6	40	Simple religious stories about the prophets
5	Parents	90	Religious ethics from traditions

The curriculum is very well organized and harmonized by the
religious leader who arranges the lessons weekly and meets with the
teachers beforehand to instruct them on how to conduct the lessons.
Toward the end of the year, these lessons are collected to be followed in Sunday school in the years to come. The teachers are ex-
clusively second-generation young women, some of whom are the product of mixed marriages.
The four small classes start in the basement from 10:00 a.m.
until 11:30 to noon. This arrangement is to give the religious leaders a chance to supervise the classes. In return, it gives the teachers and older children a chance to hear lectures about Islamic ethics.
All the classes and lectures are given in English. About noon,
all the attendants, from three generations, are engaged in the Sunday

noon prayer, lining up behind the religious leader in a traditional
way; females are at the end of the group. After the classes and lecture, there is a collection. This collection has the function of
teaching the youth how to support their mosque. It is also a borrowed
element from the American churches.

Chanting the prayer loudly at Sunday noon is a kind of adjust-
ment to the American environment. Its practical function is to teach
the youth how to perform prayer. Sunday noon prayer itself, as it
is done in the Toledo community, represents a kind of over-all religious integration with the American environment. It fills the religious vacuum in the spirit of those youths who see their friends
and schoolmates belonging and going to a church of which they are
proud. Now, they too have a God to fill their entity, to Whom they
bow and kneel, and from Whose unlimited power they derive their power
to conquer problems of everyday life. The mosque institution plays
a vital role in the life functions integrate the individual personality with that of the surrounding society.

There is also an Arabic school held every Thursday evening at
the mosque from 7 to 8:30. This school has three classes, with the
following distribution:

Table 59
ARABIC SCHOOL IN TOLEDO, BY GRADES AND AGE DISTRIBUTION

CLASS	NO. OF STUDENTS	AGE OF STUDENTS
1	15	Adults, 17+
2	10	10-16
3	25	5-9

The Arabic language is an inseparable part of Islam. As the
religious leader puts it, "It is a must for all Moslems to know some
Arabic...for religious reasons." This is the prevailing pattern in
the community. Arabic language as well as Arabic activities are
employed to serve the religious goals. The community's emphasis
is on religion. Occassionally, some Arab diplomats are invited to
help raise the social prestige of the Moslem community (see the Toledo Blade, December 6, 1958).

The mosque institution in Toledo has three seperate branches
and organizations:

Men's Branch	120 members meet once a month on Sunday
Women's Auxiliary	60 members meet twice a month on Wednesday
Youth Club	40 members meet twice a month on Monday

The Toledo Youth Organization is under the Islamic Youth Association, which is sponsored by the Islamic Federation. The Toledo
Youth Organization issues a monthly paper, edited and printed in
the Toledo mosque, for all the Youth Organizations in the United
States and Canada.

DOCUMENT 39 - 1959

"TOLEDO MOSLEMS OBSERVE RAMADAN"
30-Day Fasting Period Started

Source: The Toledo Blade, March 12, 1959.

Members of the Toledo Moslem Community have begun their annual
30-day period of fasting in observance of Ramadan, a solemn season
which commemorates the beginning of the Moslem faith through the
prophet Muhammad.

Rules of the fast provide for abstinence from food, drink and
other physical pleasures from sunrise (it is from dawn) to sunset
daily. The fast will conclude April 8.

Ramadan also is the name of the ninth month in the Islamic
calendar.

Imam Kamil Avdich, leader of the Toledo community which has
about 300 families, explained that the rigid requiremnents of the
fast provide "a way to elevate ourselves spiritually and to prove
that the human body is not the master, but servant of the human
spirit."

DOCUMENT 40 - 1959

NASSER DONATES TO U.S. MOSLEMS
Two Midwesterners Fulfill Mission
in Cairo -- Imams Will Be Sent to
Teach

Source: New York Times, September 20, 1959, p.21.

By Jay Walz, Special to the New York Times, Cairo, Sept. 12 --
    A fortnight ago two Midwesterners came here on a mission for
the 80,000 Moslems in the United States and Canada.
    They were returning today with a donation of L20,000 Egyptian
(about $50,000) from President Gamal Abdel Nasser of the United Arab
Republic toward a new Islamic center in Detroit.
    No less important, they had the promise that at least four Arab
imams would go to the United States to instruct and lead American Moslems in their prayers.
    "After we built new mosques in seven cities, we found there
were not enough imams in America to serve them," one of the visitors
said.
    An imam is a Moslem religious leader, who must undergo many years
fo study in the history, customs and theology of Islam before his
assignment to a mosque.

One a Restuarant Owner
    The two Americans are James Kalil, 37 years old, a captain on
the sheriff's force in Wayne County, Michigan, and Casim Olwan, 35,
who owns a restaurant in downtown Toledo. They are the president a
and past president, respectively, of the Federation of American Moslems, an association of Moslem societies in the United States and Canada.
    Both are American-born sons of Arab parents. Both came out of
World War II as sergeants in the United States Army. Both have under-
taken, as a principal avocation, an effort to make "good Moslems"
of all believers of that faith in the land of their families" adoption.
    Mr. Kalil said that President Nasser, in a two-hour interview,
had expressed great interest in the extend of Moslem worship in
North America. He was told that Moslems were to be found in thirty-
nine states and in five provinces of Canada.
    There are mosque-supporting communities in New York, Chicago,
Detroit, Toledo, Cedar Rapids, Iowa; Michigan City, Indiana, and in
London and Edmonton, Canada. A mosque is under construction in Gary,
Indiana.
    The search for imams brought the pair to Cairo because the capi-
tal is the seat of the ancient Islamic university, Al Azhar. This
institution was founded 1000 years ago as a center of Islamic learning.

Holds 10,000 Students
    Its dust-laden sandstone buildings just off the musky (grand
bazaar) in Old Cairo hold 10,000 students from all Moslem countries.

Graduates carry back to their home lands knowledge of sciences, arts
and culture. Many also fan out to minister to the Moslem faithful
wherever they may be.

Mr. Kalil and Mr. Olwan advised Dr. Nour El Hassan, vice rector
of Al Azhar, that seven Moslem communities in the United States and
Canada were prepared to pay travel expenses and guarantee to support
qualified imams who were willing to begin careers in "a new world."
Dr. El Hassan promised "to send us four within the next month and
three or four more later on," they said.

Imam candidates must undergo rigid competitive examinations.
They must prove themselves not only as scholars, but also as fluent
in both Arabic and English. They must possess singing voices good
enough to chant prayers from the Koran in the traditional manner.

The proposed $250,000 Islamic center in Detroit is to serve
the same educational and cultural purposes as the center erected
a few years ago in Washington, D.C.

Most American Moslems, Mr. Kalil said, are city residents, but
many live in small towns and farms in remote parts of the West and
in Northwest Canada.

"It will be impossible to send an imam to them," he explained.
"But we discussed here plans to send some of the young people there
to Cairo, perhaps to Al Azhar, to study the religion of the families
and ancestors so they can go home and help perpetuate good Moslem
observance in generations to come."

DOCUMENT 41

"MESSAGE OF THE PRESIDENT OF THE NATIONAL ASSOCIATION OF
FEDERATIONS OF SYRIAN AND LEBANESE AMERICAN CLUBS ON THE
OCCASION OF THE 1959 OVERSEAS CONVENTION."

Source: The National Herald, 1959, February
Official Organ of the N.A.F.A.L.A.C.

Again we are engaged in an Overseas Convention to Lebanon, Syria, now the Northern Region of the United Arab Republic and the other
countries of the Middle East. It is significant to note that this will
be the third such undertaking under the auspices of our organization,
the two previous conventions having been held in 1950 and 1955.

We want out conventioners to enjoy this trip back to the land
of our ancestors to the highest degree. And if past experience is
any guide, there will be much that will give us pleasure and enjoy-
ment; such as, returning to our ancestral villages, meeting our relatives and friends, attending the festivities, banquets and social
affairs arranged for us by the respective governments and by our Association, and touring and visiting historical and Biblical places
of interest.

But as much as we want all the conventioners to enjoy themselves, we should make the trip with a deep sense of responsibility
and duty both to our country and to the countries of our origin.
For, each one of us is, in a certain sense of the word, an ambassador of goodwill and friendship from our United States to our old
homelands. By our words and deeds, we can do much to reestablish
and cement the friendship, understanding and goodwill that should exist between the Arab countries and America. We must convey to our
Arab cousins, most strongly, that we are mindful of our common ancestry and cultural heritage and that we understand their problems,
and by reassuring them of the very real sympathy and genuine respect
which we and our government have for them.

Accordingly, we must take it upon ourselves to learn of their
hopes and their aspirations, and to note their progress in every way
in which they have made advancements so that, upon our returning
home, we may tell with authority our neighbors and friends what we
have seen.

Thus we will be making a valuable contribution to strengthening
the relations between the United States and the countries we visit.

Cosmo M. Ansara, President

DOCUMENT 42

ST. JUDE'S HOSPITAL AND ALSAC (1963)

Source: Philip Harsham, "Arabs in America: A Special Contribution",
Aramco World Magazine, March-April, 1975.

Arab-Americans in some of their more self-deprecating moods like
to day that no two of them ever really got together on anything--
unless it was an agreement to disagree. But that isn't altogether
true, and St. Jude Children's Research Hospital sits in Memphis, Tenn.,
as testimony to that fact. For St. Jude's while it is international,
interracial, and non-sectarian, has provided the greatest single ral-
lying point for the Arab-American community; they know that without
their help its rocketing expenses -- roughly $5,000,000 this year --
might never be met.

St. Jude's, named for the patron saint of the hopeless, was
founded by Danny Thomas, the Lebanese-American entertainer. Its
sole mission is to conduct clinical research into catastrophic mal-
adies affecting children - primarily leukemia and malnutrition - and
eradicating them. In operation only 12 years, it's scoring well:
roughly 51 percent of the children it's treated for acute lymphocytic
leukemia, starting in 1968, have been free of all evidence of the
disease for five to six years. That's the form of leukemia most prev-
alent among children, the form that 10 years ago meant almost certain death within a year. In its fight against malnutrition, in a
demonstration area where the infant mortality rate was the country's
highest, St. Jude's and a cooperating agency have reduced that rate
from 8.4 deaths per 100 births to less than one per 100 - and at a
cost of less than $100 per year per child. The St. Jude's staff is
working, too, on treatments for retinoblastoma, the cancer that causes
most childhood blindness, and on ways to stem epidemics of influenza.

And it all began with Danny Thomas in 1940. Practically desti-
tute, his career seemingly stymied, Thomas turned to St. Jude Thad-
deus. "Help me find my place in life," he prayed, "And I will build
you a shrine dedicated to the hopeless, the helpless, and the poor."
Next day, so the story goes, he was given a small part in a sales
promotion film. It was his start toward the top, and a few years
later Thomas was ready to fulfill his promise.

Deciding with the help of arch-bishop that the promised shrine
should be a hospital - something practical and needed - Thomas began
laying plans for financing it. A good starting point was the Association of Lebanese-Syrian-American Clubs (ALSAC), the widespread
social organization in which his friends were many. Its leaders
were willing to cooperate, and ALSAC - now standing for Aiding Leu-
kemia-Stricken American Children - became the name of the St. Jude's
fund-raising arm. Now headquartered in Indianapolis, Ind., it was
headed by the late Lebanese-American Michael Tamer.

ALSALC sponsors door-to-door solicitations by teenagers that
bring in about $1,500,000 each year. And through benefit banquets,
at which Danny Thomas and his Hollywood friends usually entertain,
it nets considerably more. One held in Miami, where a number of

successful Arab-Americans are concentrated, can be counted on for as much as $200,00 each year, for instance. But for the most part funds come as annual donations from individual families scattered across the country - families with names such as Ajhar, Jamail, Coury, Maykel, Ayoub, Harris, Haggar, Elias, Maloof, and Karam, to name a few. And enough comes in to account for 55 percent of the hospital's needs. The remainder is covered by foundation grants and by federal funds. For no parent of a St. Jude's patient is asked to pay a penny for his child's treatment, nor, says Danny Thomas, will ever be.

Members of the Arab-American community talk a lot about St. Jude's and the good it's doing for children. A few of the more active ones have even talked a bit about the good it's doing for them.

DOCUMENT 43 - 1969

"THE DRUZE'S ROLE IN AMERICA TODAY"

By Abdallah E. Najjar

Source: Action, English-Arabic Newpaper, New York, N.Y., June 9, 1969.

"On the question of "Who am I?" -- the questions of "What am I?" and "What is Druism?" the question of my identity and my affiliation, and the question of my roots and my belonging within the framework of American society, which we adopted and which we adopted and which has adopted us; and the question of a Druze's role in America today...

In answer to a question, "Who am I?" -- let me say, as a Druze I am a mystic in temperament -- a pragmatist by necessity -- an idealist by choice -- a Republican in theory -- and a Democrat in practice (or vice versa)...As a Druze I am Moslem influenced by oriental theology and Western thought, by Christian witness, Judaic law and esoteric practice...

The Druze in America, bewildered as he may seem to be, is rightfully attempting to cope with his existential anxiety by having the 'courage to be' -- a self affirmation in spite of the threatened possibility of non-being.

Today, we as Americans and descendants of these (Druze) people, are privileged to be able to share young and old in a probing dialogue just as others do...to pursue change in the name of God the Compassionate, the Merciful. In the pursuit of such change, we must learn and we must teach that change is never comfortable, but it is the price of growth and it is also the source of renewal.

With faith and knowledge bound together, we can hope to cherish and protect those values, those dogmas and those treasures of a heritage that we carried from the East and blended with the best of the West.

(Mr. Najjar is the Chief of International Affairs section of National Communicable Disease Center of U.S. Public Health in Atlanta, Georgia).

DOCUMENT 44 - 1971

"GEORGE A. HAMID, A GIANT OF A LEGEND
DIES AT THE AGE OF 75"

Source: Action, English-Arabic Newpaper, New York, N.Y., August 9,
1971.

Atlantic City, N.J.   George A. Hamid, Sr., operator of Steel Pier
and a show business giant, died in Atlantic City. He was 75.
     Mr. Hamid, who performed as a boy acrobat for pennies in the
streets of Lebanon, where he was born, came to America to build a
massive show business empire. He was an entertainment business ty-
coon who commanded the respect of the mightiest.
     Until his death he worked too swiftly for his secretaries as he
stood with telephone clenched in his strong hands arranging aerial
acts, animal thrillers and beautiful extravaganzas for circuses,
fairs, shopping center openings and charitable events.
     In his steel-trap mind were catalogued the addresses and tele-
phone numbers of his far-flung contacts. He spoke to proud and daring performers with a respect that was part of his inbred love for
the world of vaudeville.
     Writers searched for new superlatives to describe Hamid in fea-
tures across the nation. His many experiences and achievements, however, dwarfed all attempts to fictionalize his legend.
     Hamid's formal education consisted of three grades in primitive
schools in his native Broumana, Lebanon, but he could dictate a
lengthy publicity release that a self-respecting newsman could sub-
mit to his editor practically verbatim.
     In 1967, the U.S. Information Agency taped an interview with
Hamid for showing in at least 15 Arabic-speaking countries...Serving
as host, Hamid told in Arabic how he learned tumbling in the streets
of his Lebanese village and at the age of 9 joined his uncle's acro-
batic act with the Buffalo Bill Circus in Marseilles, France.
     Buffalo Bill (William Cody) taught him show business and Annie
Oakley tutored him in reading and writing.
     A year later he arrived in the United States...Because of his
strength as a boy Hamid was the "understander" or bottom man in the
pyramid formations of a tumbling team. When he was 13 he became the
world's champion acrobat at Madsion Square Garden.
     By the time he was 17, Hamid owned his own acrobatic act and the
highlight of his career as a performer was playing Steel Pier.
     In 1920 he started the booking agency that brought him wealth
and recognition throughout the United States and Canada. In an ordinary year he supplied more than 300 fairs, 200 local celebrations,
and 35 amusement parks with entertainment...
     In 1945 he acquired control of Steel Pier in Atlantic City. He
was the first man in history to head both Steel Pier and Million Dollar Pier at the same time.
     The rest is recent history...a parade of famous names, Benny
Goodman, the Dorsey Brothers, Frank Sinatra, Danny Kaye, etc...
some starting their careers on the famous pier.

Through it all, however, Hamid never lost the thrill of show business. He remembered every bit of it, starting from the time his uncle Ameen Ben Hamid, took him by the hand and showed the youngster all the glitter and pomp of the old world as they performed before the crowned heads of Europe.

DOCUMENT 45 - 1972

U.S. CHECKS ARABS TO BLOCK TERROR

Source: "Residents and Travelers are being Screened to Protect Israelis in the Country", New York Times, October 5, 1972, p.1.

Washington, October 4 -- The Nixon Administration, acting on a promise
by the President to protect Israeli citizens in the United States
from terrorist attacks, has begun a major effort to identify Arabs
residing in this country who are suspected of planning terrorism and
to screen travelers from Arab nations more carefully.

A spokesman for the Immigration and Naturalization Service, calling the operation "a very touchy one," declined today to elaborate
on what steps were being taken to pinpoint potential terrorists and
which Federal agencies, besides his own, were involved.

Nationwide in Scope

But other Government sources said that the effort was nation-
wide in scope and that all Federal agencies involved with international travel and with the suppression of terrorist activities were
taking part, including the State Department and the Federal Bureau
of Investigation.

Checks with Immigration Service offices in several sections of
the United States indicated that the effort was getting under way.

Mr. Nixon's statement promising to take "adequate security measures" to protect Israelis living or traveling in the United States
was made Sept. 5, the day 11 members of the Israeli Olympic team
were killed as a result of an attack by Arab guerrillas in Munich,
West Germany.

Sol Marks, a district director of the Immigration and Naturalization Service in New York, emphasized that the Government effort
aimed at preventing similar incidents in the United States focused
only on individuals the Government had reason to believe might be
planning terrorism.

No Harassment Intended

He stressed that the Government had no intention of harassing
the Arab community in general, and wished to avoid touching off a
panic among Arab students and others with legitimate reasons for being in this country.

Other Government sources indicated that the operation, about
which they refused to give details for fear of diminishing its effectiveness, had only been in effect for a day or two.

But employes in the office of the Arab Information Center here,
which is affiliated with the League of Arab States, said they had
been aware of F.B.I. surveillance for about 10 days.

Abdul el-Abyad, the center's press officer, said that almost
always in recent days there had been two unmarked cars filled with
men he believed were Federal agents parked in front of his office.

"Wherever we drive, they shadow us," he said. "We are exreme-
ly resentful of this. We regard it as obnoxious in a country under
the rule of law."

Interrogation Reported

An Arab League official, who asked not to be identified said
he had been followed while driving to and from work. Last week, he
said, he stopped his car in a Washington suburb and a car following
him stopped behind him. Two men got out, walked up to his car and
identified themselves as F.B.I. agents, he said.

"They took me to their office, took my picture and my finger-
prints and interrogated me, " he said. "They said, 'You are terrorists, you are planning violence' -- they made some kind of threat
that if something should ever happen all of you will be in trouble,
things like that."

The official, a Palestinian, said he knew of one other person
in his office who had a similar experience, as had other friends,
chiefly students and professors in the Washington area. But he refused to give any names or otherwise identify them beyond saying
that they, too, were all Palestinians.

An F.B.I. spokesman would not comment on the allegations, cit-
ing the bureau's policy of not discussing any investigation it might
be undertaking.

The Immigration Service said it could not immediately say pre-
cisely how many Arab nationals were traveling or living temporarily
in the United States. The State Department estimated the number of
Arab students here at about 6,300.

Besides surveillance and interrogation operations, which are
said to be aimed at known or suspected members of the Black September and Al Fatah groups, and their sympathizers, the Government has
recently tightened visa requirements for all foreigners in transit
through this country.

The Federal order requiring transit visas, even for foreigners
changing planes at United States airports, took effect September 27.

Noting "the general increased threat of terrorist activities
in the United States" and indications that such activities might be
planned during the current session of the United Nations General
Assembly, the order revoked until Jan. 1, 1973, the previous regula-
tion that had allowed foreigners passing through this country to
remain here for up to 10 days without a visa.

Mr. Marks noted with satisfaction the move to suspend the regu-
lation, which he said had been "a perfect vehicle for terrorists."

Under the old measure, he said, a terrorist could have committed
an act of terrorism upon arriving here and then left the country
immediately, with no way for Federal authorities to restrict or record his entry.

There have been no known acts of terrorism attributable to
Arab groups in this country so far, but three letters containing
small but deadly bombs were discovered in a New York post office
last month.

The bombs were like others mailed to Israeli diplomats abroad,
including one that exploded and killed an Israeli Embassy official
in London. Another letter-bomb intercepted in London before it
exploded carried a note signed with the name Black September, the
organization claiming responsibility for the Munich killings.

DOCUMENT 46 - 1972

LETTER TO PRESIDENT RICHARD M. NIXON

From M. Cherif Bassiouni, past President
of the AAUG (Association of Arab-American
University Graduates) - Regarding "Operation Boulder"

Source: Information Paper Number 10, January, 1974, Association of
Arab-American University Graduates, Inc., North Dartmouth, Mass.

On Thursday, October 5, 1972, the New York Times reported that
on special instructions from the White House, "Arab residents in the
United States would be the subject of special measures taken by several cases in Chicago, Boston and Detroit where FBI agents have ha-
rassed citizens and residents of Arab origin under the pretense that
they are under special instructions from Washington.
    This policy of singling out an ethnic community as a targe for
"special measures" of this sort is clearly in violation of the Constitution and laws of this country and is too reminiscent of the early
treatment of Japanese Americans during World War II.
    That an American ethnic group can be singled out because of
their heritage to be the object of harassment sends ripples of shock
throughout all heritage groups and is indeed abhorrent to all Americans, as I am sure it would be to you.
    As a responsible member of this community and, above all, as an
American Citizen, I feel compelled to bring this matter to your personal attention and to urge you to examine this new policy.

The reply came from FBI Acting Director L. Patrick Gray III on Novem-
l, 1972, wherein he stated:
    I do not know details of the cases brought to your attention,
    but I can assure you the Federal Bureau of Investigation has
    not embarked upon a policy of singling out any ethnic community
    as a target for "special measures." The Federal Bureau of In-
    vestigation does not investigate threats to the internal securi-
    ty of the United States. National origin or citizenship of the
    individuals involved is not a criterion for initiating investi-
    gation; however, membership in or affiliated with organizations
    reliably reported to be engaged in subversive activity against
    the security of the United States is a sufficient reason for
    inquiry regarding the individual so involved.
    With specific reference to investigations of individuals of Ara-
    bic origin, I wish to emphasize that such investigations are not
    based upon any ethnic factor. The investigations are based
    soley upon membership or activity in organizations which have
    been reliable reported to threaten the internal security of
    the United States.

DOCUMENT 47 - 1972

LETTER TO ATTORNEY GENERAL RICHARD KLEINDIENST

From Aryeh Neier, Executive Director
of the American Civil Liberties Union
October 16, 1972, Regarding "Operation Boulder"

Source: Information Paper Number 10, January 1974, Association of
Arab-American University Graduates, Inc., North Dartmouth, Mass.
    The American Civil Liberties Union has received reports about
the special measures being taken by several federal agencies, particularly the Federal Bureau of Investigation and the Immigration and
Naturalization service, against resident Arabs. Apparently, the
purpose of these measures is to forestall acts of terrorism against
Israeli citizens and American Jews.
    While terrorist incidents abroad make it clear that the govern-
ment interests here are important, the measures reportedly being taken
by the several federal agencies give the appearance of dragnet investi-
gations based solely upon an individual's national origin. If that
impression is accurate, they must be condemned as constitutionally
impermissible insofar as they go beyond fair and respectful inquiries
by law enforcement officers for the purpose of securing voluntary
information about the planning or commission of crimes.
    But the reports we have received suggest that federal officers
are going beyond the limit of neutral inquiry, and are engaging in
a visible course of investigation, interrogation and surveillance
of members of a specific national group which has the effect of harassing and intimidating them. That in itself is to be condemned; beyond that, however, the law enforcement activities have generated
the impression in the Arabic community that public statements of support for the Arabic position in the Arab-Israeli dispute will be reason enough for federal officers to take an official interest in the
effect of discouraging the expression of such views with the conse-
quent impairment of rights protected -- to resident aliens as much
as to citizens -- by the First Amendment...
    To single out any group on the basis of national origin, race,
political beliefs or religion as a target for criminal investigation
is objectionable from a constitutional point of view and treads upon
the presumption of innocence. We urge that you issue the instructions
we have set out above and reassure the Arabic community that their
civil liberties are not to be violated because of their national origin.

DOCUMENT 48 - 1973

"REPRESENTATIVE D.V. DANIELS LAUDS
JERSEY CITY'S EGYPTIAN COMMUNITY"

Source: Reprinted from the Congressional Record, June, 1973.

Washington, D.C. -- Representative Dominick V. Daniels of N.J. recently made the following statement in the House of Representatives
regarding the activities of the growing Egyptian community which
makes its home in Jersey City, N.J. It is being reprinted from the
Congressional Record.
    Mr. Speaker, Hudson County, N.J., which I have the honor to
represent in this House is famous for the number of ethnoreligious
and ethnic groups which dwell in harmony together, often despite
serious divisions on the other side.
    Mr. Speaker, one of the most interesting groups of people who
live in the 14th Congressional District is the Egyptian descended
community. Both Coptic Christians and Moslems live in my Congressional District and I am happy to say they live in harmony with
each other and the rest of the people who make up the mosaic of Jersey City and Hudson County.
    Mr. Speaker, everyone in Hudson County is impressed with the
Egyptian community. They are hardworking people who like many immigrants who came before them simply wish to improve their lot in
life through their own efforts. They are a welcome addition to
Hudson County.
    Because so many Members may not be familiar with the Egyptian
people I ask that a most interesting article from the May 30, 1973
edition of the Jersey Journal be reprinted at this point in the Record.
    The article follows: JERSEY CITY'S EGYPTIAN COLONY FINDS
PEACE, SECURITY, JOBS
    They come to Jersey City from New York, Philadelphia, Los An-
geles, Cairo and Alexandria.
    All of them have college degrees; yet many live here because
the rents are low enough to support a family on a security guard's
salary.
    Jersey City's estimated 5,000 Egyptians have come to America
not as refugees from poverty or war, but because they see America
as a land of unlimited opportunity.
    "In Egypt," observes Mohamed Elsa, a cost accountant, who lives
here and works in New York, "life is simple and you can live cheap-
ly. In America, life is hard and expensive, but you have the freedom to make as much money as you want. You pay taxes, the rest is
yours."
    In Egypt a professional worker is paid a fixed salary by the
government.
    Elsa works at a job for thich he received training in Egypt.
Abouel Kier Gad, who came to America two and a half years ago armed
with an engineering degree, has, like many Egyptians, found his degree virtually useless.

But, like many Egyptians, he is holding down two jobs and saving his money for the future when he will take enough graduate courses to make his degree operative.

"America is a fine place," Gad says eagerly, speaking across the counter of the small grocery he owns on Kennedy Boulevard. "Here you can make all you want."

Adel Morgan, an agricultural engineer, came to America four years ago. He heard that New Jersey was called "the Garden State" and he settled in Jersey City because he thought he could "work in the gardens."

He is now a supervisor in a Newark plastics company.

Morgan says he came to America for the same reason the colonists came to America, for opportunity.

When he is asked what he does in his spare time, Morgan explodes with laughter.

"We have no time!" he says. "Here in America you have to keep running all the time to make a living."

All the Egyptian men queried about leisure activities said they have no time for leisure.

Since 1965 several thousand Egyptians have settled in Jersey City. The city's proximity to New York, where many of them work, is the reason first given by Egyptians as to why they choose to live here.

Since many hold down menial jobs while attending graduate school, they can live in low-rent districts with more safety than they could have in comparable neighborhoods in New York.

Abouel Gad, who was mugged twice when he lived in the Williamsburg section of Brooklyn says "it is nice here - quiet." He says New York is too dangerous for his children.

Recent immigrants chose Jersey City because they already have friends, relatives and a place to worship here.

Jersey City has a storefront Moslem mosque at 2326 Kennedy Boulevard and a Coptic Orthodox Church at 427 West Side Ave.

The Copts and the Moslems -- who have been at odds in Egypt for nearly 2,000 years -- are at peace in America.

"We cannot get away with fighting here," says Abouel Gad, a Copt, who claims to have twenty-five Moslem friends. "In America, we are Egyptians. We attend different churches, but we are brothers."

Mohamed Elsa says that there is one disadvantage of living in America:

"In America there is great wealth but little humanity. In Egypt it is the opposite.

"Here everyone is independent. They mind their own business, that's it."

Elsa says he thinks the "lack of humanity" is the reason crime is rampant in America.

"There is little crime in Egypt, Elsa says, "because there the pace is slow, and we have time to care for each other."

DOCUMENT 49 - 1973

STATEMENT OF PRINCIPLE AND OBJECTIVES:
THE NATIONAL ASSOCIATION OF ARAB AMERICANS

Source: Washington, D.C., Preamble, The National Association of
Arab Americans.

We, Americans of Arab Ancestry conscious of our responsibilities as
citizens of this democracy, to preserve and maintain the high principles upon which it was established, including self-determination and
justice for all peoples, and proud of our Arab heritage, which has
contributed so richly to world civilization and development, and
is devoted to the highest ideal of democracy, peace, justice and brotherhood of man, as set forth in the Charter of the United Nations, do
hereby form this Association for the objectives herein set forth:

OBJECTIVES

1. To foster, encourage and promote the traditional
   ties between the people of the United States and
   the people of the Arab countries.
2. To engage in political, social, cultural and educational activities for the prupose of maintaining political action and involvement in the United
   States.
3. To give support and assistance to citizens of Arab
   ancestry throughout the United States to assist
   them in any endeavor to attain positions of local,
   state and national office.
4. To support and assist members of Congress and others
   in the U.S. government who support the objectives
   of the N.A.A.A.
5. To maintain official communications with the appro-
   priate officials in Washington, D.C., the United
   Nations and elsewhere in the continental limits of
   the U.S.A.
6. To exchange opinions, formulate plans, conduct dialogue for the avowed prupose of encouraging better
   relations between the U.S.A. and the Arab countries.

FOUNDERS:
George Hismeh, Dr. Assad Khoury, Mahmoud Sadak, Dick
Shadyac, Dr. Hisham Sharabi, Fuad Taima.
OFFICERS:
Dr. Peter S. Tanous, President
Edmond Howar, Vice President
Dr. William Driebe, Treasurer
Michael Saah, Secretary

DOCUMENT 50 - 1973

DELEGATION REPRESENTING NATIONAL ASSOCIATION
OF ARAB-AMERICAN MEETS WITH SECRETARY OF STATE

Source: Action, Arabic-English Newspaper, Inc., May 7, 1973, p.4.

Washington D.C., - Dr. Peter Tanous, President of the National Association of Arab Americans, on April 16, 1973 led a delegation which
met with the Secretary of State, Mr. William P. Rogers. Accompany-
ing Dr. Tanous was Mr. Woodrow W. Woody, of Detroit, Michigan and
Mr. Minor George of Cleveland, Ohio. The meeting took place in
the office of the Secretary at 3:30 P.M.
    A prepared statement outling the strong feelings of the Arab
American Community throughout the United States, was presented to
Secretary Rogers.
    Secretary Rogers thanked the delegation for coming and expressed
his pleasure at having an opportunity to talk with them.
    Dr. Tanous, in a very frank and open discussion asked the Secre-
tary when and where the U.S. planned to draw the line and take some
action to halt future incursions into Lebanon and other Arab countries
by Israel; and, was the U.S. prepared to prevent Israel from occupy-
ing any of Lebanon's territory. Mr. Rogers' answer was this, "The
United States has always, and continues to guarantee the territorial
integrity of Lebanon." In answer to a question raised regarding the
use of the veto by the U.S. in the United Nations Security Council
meeting, Mr. Rogers indicated that the U.S. would support a balanced
resolution referring to both Israeli agression and Arab terrorism.
However, it would not support a unilateral condemnaticn of either
side; to which Dr. Tanous responded, "Our government is equating the
actions of two entirely different entities -- one an isolated group
of frustrated individuals, and the other is an accepted Nations recognized by the world community. To condemn all Arab Nations because
of the actions of a few frustrated individuals, would approximate
condemning all Blacks in the U.S. for the Black Panters actions at
San Jose, California when Judge Hoyle was murdered."
    In response to a question as to what the U.S. policy was toward
the Palestinian refugees, Mr. Rogers stated that this was a great
problem, and "the rights of the Palestinian must be considered in any
Middle East settlement, if the settlement is to be a lasting one."
    Question by Dr. Tanous: "The Arab Nations had, in general, ac-
cepted the 'Rogers Plan', Israel has not. Why not apply pressure to
Israel to accept?" Secretary Rogers answered , "A forced settlement
will not produce a lasting peace. We are striving for an agreement
that is acceptable to both parties." To which Dr. Tanous responded,
"This concept is good, but it never works, for neither side will
relinquish what it believes to be valid points. The U.S. could apply
pressure on Israel by restricting shipments of phantoms and other
sophisticated weaponry. But the important thing is that action must
be taken to start negotiations moving at the earliest possible date."
    The Secretary apologized for the fact that he could not spend
more time with the delegation, since he had been called to a meeting

with the President at the White House. He did, however, assure Dr. Tanous that he would take the statement home with him and read it carefully.

The delegates were encouraged by their meeting with the Secretary of State and intend to continue to maintain a dialogue with the Department of State and other agencies of the government.

DOCUMENT 51 - 1974

"ARAB LEADER DEPLORES THE ARSON"

Source: New York Post, June 4, 1974, p.6.

The head of the Action Committee on American Arab Relations stood outside his fire-blackened offices on E. 43rd Street and discussed civil liberties.

"I despise these things, " said Dr. M.T. Mehdi of the fire, which the Fire Department said was deliberately set, "not so much because of destruction of property, but because of their (the arsonist's) evil attempts to suppress our freedom of speech."

Mehdi is the city's most prominent Arab spokesman and was recently hospitalized with three fractured vertebrae following an attack by unknown assailants after a pro-Israeli demonstration at the U.N.

The unknow arsonist hit his office yesterday morning.

FIRE UNDER INVESTIGATION--

"It's a set fire that is under investigation," said Fire Marshal James McCormack.

A spokesman for the pro-Arab group said an offset press and addressograph machine and "important documents which cannot be replaced" were lost in the fire which destroyed three rooms on the third floor at 4E. 43rd Street. Mehdi estimated their loss at $400,000.

The rest of the third floor, also occupied by the organization, was damaged by smoke and water.

These "hoodlums think they have the right to supress our freedom of speech," said Mehdi. "We shall not be intimidated. We shall go on."

Mehdi blamed the Jewish Defense League for the fire and the other actions against his organization. He also was critical of Mayor Beame.

"We charge the J.D.L. and other pro-Israeli groups -- based on their previous record of violence," he said and added, "We feel that Mayor Abraham Beame has at least an indirect responsibility for this expansion of violence against the Arabs in the city. Beame has been attacking Arab people in his speeches -- encouraging those thugs to take the law into their hands."

DOCUMENT 52 - 1975

"HISTORICAL GLIMPSE OF THE AMERICAN
ARABIC SPEAKING COMMUNITY PRESS"

Source: 1975 Almanac, Joseph R. Haiek, Editor-Publisher, published
annually by The News Circle, Los Angeles, California.

Without doubt, any intellectual society is measured by its
press and literature. With the number of the immigrants growing rapidly, the pioneer thinkers of the American-Arabic Speaking community
at the turn of the century felt the need and the motivation to form
its own press.

These intellectuals did not lose time to take advantage of the
American freedom of the press after their Ottoman persecution and its
strict censorship of the written word. They expressed their beliefs
freely without fear of repression, stimulated the sense of responsibility and pride, helped preserve the Arabic heritage and language,
promoted business opportunities, announced social and cultural events,
reported community and back-home news, and offered citizenship guidance.

Arabic typesetting machines were imported from Egypt. The first
Arabic newpaper, Kawkab America, was published in 1892 by Dr. Najeeb
Arbeely, who also was the first Syrian appointed to the US Immigration
Department. Al Ayam followed soon after. It was founded in 1897 by
Joseph Malouf.

Naoum Moukarzel founded Al Hoda on February 22, 1898, in Philadelphia. Then, in 1903, he moved the offices to New York, which had
the largest concentration of immigrants. Salloum Mokarzel, who was
publishing the "Al Majallah Al Tujariah" and "The Syrian World,"
published in English, took over the ownership of Al Hoda following
the death of his brother, Naou, in 1932. Salloum was able to keep
Al Hoda in circulation despite the economic difficulties of the thir-
ties. In 1952, Salloum died, leaving Al Hoda to his eldest daughter,
Mary, who was always very close to her father, assisting him by being his secretary, consultant and nurse.

Al Hoda entered its third phase of ownership and Mary continued
its traditional policy in spite of many hardships. In 1954, Mary
Mokarzel acquired the Lebanese American Journal, published in English
to serve the needs of the community members who did not read Arabic.

Fares Stephen, in 1971, was the fourth owner and is still running both the New Al Hoda and the New Lebanese American Journal,
from New York.

Al Hoda was described by observers as "The Shrine of the Arabic
press in America." It is the oldest Arabic newpaper in the Americas,
now in its 77th year.

Dr. Philip Hitti wrote that "a census taken in 1929 lists 102
Arabic periodicals and papers which saw the light in the U.S.A."

The current community newpapers, published in major American
cities, are constantly increasing. These may be found in a variety
of sizes, frequency, Arabic and English languages and specific editorial policy.

During the seventies, the number of newspapers and radio programs significantly increased. In Los Angeles alone, in December 1974, there were five monthly newspapers.

Plans are now underway to form a national Arab-American Press organization. In this regard, The News Circle, in an editorial under the heading "Is there room to organize our Media?" wrote: "There has been much activity by the Arab-American media in recent years, but there still is no central organization to tie our media together and focus aims, methods, and ethics into a neat, comprehensive whole. What is needed is a national media organization, and the News Circle suggests as starters that such a group be established.

"Many readers probably are familiar with the many existing national organizations involving the Arab-American community, but it would be hard to name one that has worked solely toward uniting media resources into a well-knitted unit.

"The purposes: To function as a professional and educational organization comprised of the American-Arabic speaking community members engaged in the field of communication, namely journalists, editors, publishers, public relations, broadcasters, news photographers, television, motion pictures, advertising and publishing. It would include also authors, public speakers and other allied fields...

"To provide the general American media with prompt, accurate and up-to-date information about the Arab-American community. This could be done by establishing a syndicated news service capable of providing information kits to all interested media parties...

"To create a scholarship fund, encouraging community college students to prusue careers in the field of communications.

"To help foster better understanding between the Arab and the American people and provide sound communication for improved representation of the Arab-American community."...

DOCUMENT 53 - 1975

"YEMENI MIGRANT WORKERS IN CALIFORNIA"

By Mary Bisharat

Source: Arabs in America, Myths and Realities, Abu-Laban & Zeadey, Medina University Press International, 1975.

The current profile of the Yemeni farm laborer is of a young man in his twenties. His skin is deeply tanned, his frame is small and he is slender, almost underweight. He is shy, definitely wary, and hesitant to make any disclosure. He is Muslim, and though he does not observe the fast of Ramadan because of the auduous nature of his work, he prays five times a day in the field and attends the mosque whenever possible. He is married, but his wife and children have remained in Yemen. He speaks no English and makes no formal attempt to learn it. We are told that he can read and write Arabic. He is seclusive and associates with few people outside the circle of his fellow workers. He avoids any situation that might cause trouble, and to this end he polices his friends. Avoiding drinking, smoking, and public entertainment, he spends his leisure time with his fellow workers, talking and playing cards. ...The Yemini worker usually sends $1000 to $1,500 a year to his family in Yemen. This represents half his annual income...The Yemeni gets along well with his Chicano and Filipino coworkers.

DOCUMENT 54 - 1977

AROUND THE NATION
F.T.C. OFFICIAL IS ASKED FOR APOLOGY OVER NADER
WASHINGTON, JANUARY 31

Source: New York Times, February 1, 1977.

The director of the National Association of Arab Americans has
written to President Carter protesting a recent public characteriza-
tion of Ralph Nader as "a dirty Arab" by Paul Rand Dixon, a Fereral
Trade commissioner and a prime target of a Nader-sponsored report
on the F.T.C.

The letter from Michael Saba, executive director of the association, hand-delivered to the White House today, called on Mr. Carter
to "instruct Commissioner Dixon to issue a public apology for his
statement," which it said was "an outrage to every American generally and to each and every Arab-American in particular."

The name-calling, according to Mr. Saba's letter and to others
who were present took place during Mr. Dixon's appearance at a convention of the Grocery Association of America on Jan. 17 at a hotel
in Arlington, Va.

Mr. Dixon, in a telephone interview, said that his remarks were
intended to apply "only to Mr. Nader," the consumer activist, who
is of Lebanese descent, and added: "I profoundly apologize to any
Arab wherever he may be for any inference" that might be drawn from
his words concerning Arabs generally.

Mr. Nader was quoted by the Associated Press as saying "he (Mr.
Dixon) owes me and many other Americans an apology, and he will give
me one."

A spokesman fot the American Jewish Congress, calling the re-
mark about Mr. Nader deplorable, urged yesterday that Mr. Dixon "make
a public apology for his intemperate language." Richard Cohen, associate exective director of the organization, said that such "ethnic slurs should have no place in the vocabulary of governmental
policymakers."

DOCUMENT 55 - 1977

ABOUREZK CRITICIZES DIXON

Source: Abourezk News Release, February 1, 1977.

Abourezk/news release

Senator James Abourezk (D.-S.Dak.)   For further information
Senate Office Bldg.   contact: (202) 224-5842
Washington, D.C. 20510

for immediate release: Tuesday, Feb.1, 1977

ABOUREZK CRITICIZES DIXON RACIAL SLUR
Washington, D.C. -- Following FTC Commissioner Dixon's racial slur
directed toward consumer advocate Ralph Nader, South Dakota Senator
James Abourezk said, "There appears to be no ethnic group remain-
ing in America which has not been the butt of know-nothing racism
of the type manifested by Commissioner Dixon."

Abourezk said Dixon apparently lacked the decency to make a
direct apology to Ralph Nader although an apology was directed to
the National Association of Arab Americans.

APPENDICES

TABLE 1

ARAB-AMERICAN POPULATIONS OF THE VARIOUS STATES
Based primarily on incomplete surveys and on
the 1970 U.S. Census (1972 American Almanac),
the study showed the states with largest Arab-
American populations in 1970 as follows:

STATE	ARAB AMERICANS	VOTING-AGE (65% over 18)	COLLEGE GRADUATES (over 25)
California	258,000	168,000	16,800
New York	195,000	127,000	12,700
Ohio	117,000	76,000	7,600
Illinois	116,000	75,000	7,500
Pennsylvania	115,000	75.000	7,500
Michigan	95,000	64,000	6,400
Texas	90,000	59,000	5,900
Massachusetts	62,400	40,500	4,050
North Carolina	56,000	36,500	3,650
Virginia	51,000	33,000	3,300
Wisconsin	49,500	32,000	3,200
New Jersey	44,000	28,500	2,850
Florida	42,000	27,500	2,750
Maryland	39,400	25,600	2,560
Washington	37,500	24,500	2,450
Indiana	35,000	22,800	2,280
Missouri	33,000	21,500	2,150
Connecticut	30,000	19,600	1,960
Minnesota	26,000	17,000	1,700
Georgia	25,000	16,200	1,620
Louisiana	22,000	14,300	1,430
Colorado	17,400	11,400	1,140
Tennessee	16,400	10,600	1,060
Alabama	16,200	10,500	1,050
Arizona	15,800	10,000	1,000
West Virginia	15,800	10,000	1,000
Oklahoma	14,000	9,000	900
Oregon	11,500	7,500	750
Kentucky	10,200	6,600	660
D.C.	9,000	5,900	590
Iowa	9,000	5,900	590
South Carolina	9,000	5,900	590
Rhode Island	8,800	5,700	570
Kansas	8,500	5,500	550
Utah	7,800	5,000	500

TABLE 2

FIRST-GENERATION RESPONDENTS' FIRST OCCUPATIONS IN AMERICA

	Number	%
Peddler	58	40
Salesman	13	9
Business	12	8
Unskilled	28	19
Working with relatives	31	21
Farmers	4	3
Total	146	100

Source: Elkoly, Abdo A. "The Arab Moslems in the United States, Religion and Assimilation" College and University Press New Haven, Conn. 1966, P. 60.

TABLE 3

NUMBER OF ARAB IMMIGRANTS IN PROFESSIONS, 1962-1969

COUNTRY	I	II	III	IV	V	VI	TOTAL
Egypt	2,716	564	171	231	32	25	9,315
Lebanon	1,211	277	169	95	20	97	8,193
Jordan & Palestine	886	117	27	47	11	42	9,540
Iraq	774	165	45	67	4	13	4,192
Syria	463	129	43	30	5	13	2,400
Morocco	238	18	14	3	0	9	2,473
Tunisia	139	4	13	6	1	2	490
Algeria	113	9	1	2	6	1	983
Total	6,560	1,283	483	481	79	202	37,600

I- Technican

II- Engineering

III- Physician

IV- Natural Science

V- Physical Science

VI- Nurse

Source: (Al-Kindilchie, Amer Ibrahim
"Arab Immigrants in the United States:
Mougaz Al-Anbaa Press New York - 1976
p. 14 (Arabic)

TABLE 4

THE PRESS OF THE AMERICAN ARABIC-
SPEAKING COMMUNITY

Newspapers-U.S.A.

AAUG NEWSLETTER
P.O. Box 7391
North End Stn.
Detroit, Mich. 48202
by the AAUG-English

ACTION Newspaper
P.O. Box 416
New York, N.Y. 10017
Dr. M.T. Mehdi, Editor
English

AL ISLAH
260 W. Broadway
New York, N.Y. 10013
By Dr. Alphonse Chaurize
Arabic

AMERICAN-ARAB MESSAGE
17514 Woodward Ave.
Detroit, Mich. 48203

AL MISHRAQ
56 Candler
Highland Park,
Detroit, Mich. 48203
by Hanna Yatooma

ARAB TRIBUNE
302. E. Central Ave.
Toledo Ohio 43608
by Joseph Hayeck
English

BELADY
P.O. Box 1430
Glendale, Ca. 91209
by Onsi Antoun
Arabic-English

THE CEDAR PRESS
P.O. Box 14624
Long Beach, Ca. 90814
By Samir N. Nader
English

THE EGYPTIAN
P.O. Box 34059
Los Angeles, Ca. 90034
By Fouad Alkassas
Arabic, English

HATHIHE RAMALLAH
P.O. Box 116
Dearborn Heights, Mich.
48127 - By Ramalla
Federation-N. Ajlouni,
editor

THE HERITAGE
30 E. 40th St.
New York, N.Y. 10016
by Dr. N.K. Basile
English

THE MECC NEWSLETTER
255-55th St.
Brooklyn, N.Y. 11220
by the M.E. Coordinating
Cmtt. - Jim Humsie, ed.
English

NEW LEBANESE-AMERICAN
JOURNAL
16 W. 30th St.
New York, N.Y. 10001
By Fares Stephen - Engl.

THE NEWS CIRCLE
P.O. Box 74637
Los Angeles, Ca. 90004
By Joseph R. Haiek
English

AL-'ALAM AL-JADID
4003 Edgeland
Royal Oak, Mich. 48073
Yusuf Antone, Editor
Arabic & English

THE OFFICIAL BULLETIN
1206 C & I Bldg.
Houston, Texas 77002
By Southern Federation
of Syrian-Lebanese-
American Clubs-
English
Kamal Antone, Editor

THE PALESTINIAN VOICE
6513 Hollywood Bl.
Suite 207
Hollywood, Ca. 90028
by Mustafa Siam
Arabic-English

THE UNITY NEWSLETTER
P.O. Box 26225
Los Angeles, Ca. 90026
by The American-Arab
Soc.
English

THE VOICE
1028 Connecticut Ave.
NW
Washington, D.C. 20036
by Nat'l. Assoc.
Arab-Americans English

VOICE OF MASR
2824 Kennedy Blvd.
Jersey City, N.J. 07306
By Dr. William Elmiry

CARAVAN WEST
P.O. Box 18027
Rochester, N.Y. 14618
By AASR
English

AL HODA
16 W. 30th St.
New York, N.Y. 10001
by Fares Stephen
Arabic

RADIO

THE ARAB VOICE IN
DETROIT
615 Griswold - Suite 600
Detorit, Mich. 48226
By Faisal Arabo

ARABIC RADIO PROGRAM
176 W. Adams St.
Chicago, Ill. 60603
By Adel Haleem

ARABIC RADIO PROGRAM
P.O. Box 4444
San Rafael, Ca. 94903
By Wafa Darwazek

ARABESQUE RADIO PROGRAM
P.O. Box 285, Radio City Sta.
New York, N.Y. 10019
By Ghazi Khankan

ARABIC RADIO PROGRAM
1303 Prospect Ave.
Cleveland, Ohio 44115
By Abdulla Mina
on WZAK, Wed. 10 pm

MUSIC OF THE NEAR EAST
102 Hatfield St.
Pawtucket, R.I. 02861

THE VOICE OF PALESTINE
P.O. Box 5421
Chicago, Ill. 60680
By Arab American Congress
For Palestine on
WSBC - Wed. 9 P.M.

ARABIC RADIO
131 Elm St.
Wyandotte, Mich. 48192
By Sabah P. Najor

ARABIC RADIO PROGRAM
49 Audubon Rd.
Reading, Mass. 01867
Nancy Shagoury, director

CANADA - Press

ARAB DAWN
P.O. Box 9603 STE-FOY
Quebec
English-Arabic- French

ARAB CANADA
NEWSLETTER
170 Laurier W. No. 709
Ottawa, Ont. K1P 5V5
English

THE ARAB WORLD REVIEW
P.O. Box 237 Youville Sta.
Montreal H2P 2V4, Canada
By R.R. Kneider
Arabic-English-French

ASDA MARAKAH
P.O. Box 872
London, Ont.
Arabic

ASH SHARARA
P.O. Box 185 STN.
Montreal
By Arab Progressive
Study Group
English

CANADIAN MIDDLE EAST
JOURNAL
285 Jean Talon E.
Montreal, 327, Canada
By Joseph Lahoud
Arabic-English-French

FEDAYIN
1015 St. Catherine E.
Montreal, Quebec
By Rezeq Faraj
English-French

JERUSALEM TIMES
P.O. Box 65654 Stm. (F)
Vancouver, B.C. V5N 5K7
By Joseph Maleh
English-Arabic

RADIO

ARAB PRESS REVIEW-
RADIO
The Broadcasting Foundation of
America
52 Vanderbilt Ave.
New York, N.Y. 10017
A weekly 15-minute taped
digest editorial opinion
from the Arab World Press.

CANADA - Press

NEWS FROM IRAQ
377 Stewart St.
Ottawa, Ont.
Arabic

THE SOURCE
P.O. Box 992
Edmont, Alberta
By Ahmad Murad
Arabic-English

BIBLIOGRAPHY

Abu-Laban, Baha, and Zeadey, Faith T. (eds.) Arabs in America,
    Myths and Realties. The Medina University Press International,
    Wilmette, Illinois, 1975.

Abu-Laban, Baha, "The Arab-Canadian Community", in Hagopian and
    Paden, op. cit. 1969.

Abu-Laban, Sharon M., "Stereotype of Middle East People: An Anal-
    ysis of Church School Curricula, "Abu-Laban and Zeadey, op.
    cit., 1975.

Al Akl, F.M., Until Summer Comes, Pond-Ekberg Company, Springfield,
    Mass. 1945. (An autobiographical account of an Arab-American
    physician.)

Al-Kindilchie, Amer Ibrahim, Arab Immigrants in the United States.
    Mougaz Al-Anbaa Press, New York, 1976. (Arabic).

Altoma, Salih, J., "Modern Arabic Literature: A Bibliography of
    Articles, Books, Dissertations and Translations in English"
    Indiana University, Asian Studies Research Institute, Bloom-
    ington, Indiana, 1975. (This has a chapter on Mahjarite
    (Arab American) Writings.

Al-Qazzaz, Ayad, "Images of the Arab in American Social Science
    Textbooks," in Abu Laban & Zeadey, op. cit., 1975.

The American-Arabic Speaking Community Almanac, Joseph R. Haiek,
    Editor-Publisher. Published annually by The News Circle,
    P.O.B. 74637, Los Angeles, California 90004.

Anid, Cyril Rev., I Grew With Them, Paulist Press, Jounieh, Leb-
    anon, 1967. (This is the story of the assimilation of the
    Syrian Catholics of Patterson, New Jersey.

Ansara, James, "The Immigration and Settlement of the Syrians,"
    Harvard University M.A. Thesis, Cambridge, Mass., 1931.

Aramco World Magazine, published bimonthly by the Arabian American
    Oil Company, 1345 Avenue of the Americas, New York, NY 10019.

Arida and Andria, The Syrian American Directory Almanac, New York,
    N.Y. 1930 (English-Arabic), Commercial and Residential listings
    for New York City and Brooklyn.

Association of Arab-American University Graduates, "Information
    Papers, "AAUG, P.C. Box 85, North Darmouth, Mass., 02747.

Aswad, Barbara, Arabic Speaking Communities in American Cities,
    Center for Migration Studies, Staten Island, New York, 1974.

Ayoob, Joseph C., Were the Phoenicians the First to Discover America? the compiler, Aliquippa, Pennsylvania, 1950.

Benyon, E.D., "The Near East in Flint, Michigan: Assyrians and Druze and Their Antecedents, "Geographical Review. January, 1944.

Berger, Monroe, "Americans from the Arab World" in James Kritzeck and R. Bayly Winder (eds.) The World of Islam, St. Martins Press, New York, 1959.

Bisharat, Mary, "Yemeni Migrant Workers in California", Abu-Laban & Zeadey, op. cit., 1975.

Blatty, William P., Which way to Mecca, Jack? Bernard Geis Associates, New York 1960. (A humurous account of growing up in America with a Lebanese mother.)

Boland, Charles Michael, They all Discovered America, Doubleday & Company, Inc., New York, 1961.

Eilts, Hermann Frederick, Ahmad Bin Na'Aman's Mission to the United States in 1850. The Voyage of Al-Sultanah to New York City. Reprinted by the Embassy of Oman, Washington, D.C.

Elkholy, Abdo A., The Arab Moslems in the United States, College and University Press, New Haven, Conn., 1969.

Georgaskas, Dan, "Black and Arab Auto Workers in Detroit," in Abu-Laban & Zeadey, op. cit., 1975.

Gebran, Jean and Gibran, Kahlil, Kahlil Gibran, His Life and World, New York Graphic Society, Greenwhich, Conn., 1974.

Kheirallah, George, The Life of Gibran Kahlil and His Processions, New York, 1947.

Gibran, Kahlil, The Prophet, Alfred Knopf, New York, 1923.

_____. The Madman, Alfred Knopf, New York, 1918.

_____. Sand and Foam, Alfred Knopf, New York, 1926.

_____. Jesus, the Son of Man, Alfred Knopf, New York, 1928.

_____. The Earth Gods, Alfred Knopf, New York, 1931.

_____. The Garden of the Prophet, Alfred Knopf, New York 1933.

Haddad, Safia, "The Woman's Role in Socialization of Syrian-Americans in Chicago" in Hagopian and Paden, op. cit., 1969.

Hagopian, Elaine and Paden, Ann, Arab-Americans: Studies in Assimilation, Medina University Press, Wilmette, Illinois, 1969.

Hawie, Ashad G., The Rainbow Ends, Theodore Gaus Sons, New York, 1942. (Autobiographical).

Hitti, Philip, Syrians in America, George Doran, New York, 1924.

Hoar, George F. Autobiography of Seventy Years, Volume II, Scribner's Sons, New York, 1903.

Houghton, Louise, "Syrians in the United States" The Survey July 1, 1911; Aug. 5, 1911; Sept. 2, 1911; Oct. 7, 1911.

Katibah, Habib I., Arabic-Speaking Americans, The Institute of Arab-American Affiars, New York, 1946.

Kayal, Philip M. and Joseph M., The Syrian-Lebanese in America, A Study in Religion and Assimilation, Twayne Publishers, A division of G.K. Hall & Co., Boston, 1975.

Lovell, Emily, "A Survey of Arab-Muslims in the United States and Canada," Muslim World, April, 1973.

Makdisi, Nadim, "Arab Adventures into the New World". Yearbook 1965-66, The Action Committee on American-Arab Relations," New York, 1966.

Mehdi, M.T., Kennedy and Sirhan, Why? New World Press, New York, 1969.

_____. A Nation of Lions Chained, New World Press, New York, 1962. (A look at U.S. policy toward the Mid East in contrast to Lederer's A Nation of Sheep, which looked at U.S. policy toward the Far East.)

Miller, Lucius Hopkins, Our Syrian Population: A study of the Syrian population of Greater New York, 1904.

Mokarzel, Salloum, "The People of New York", Life, February 17, 1947.

Rihbany, Abraham Mitrie Rev., A Far Journey, Houghton-Mifflin Co., Boston, 1914. (An autobiographical account of this well-known Arab-American minister.)

The Syrian Charter, Houghton Mifflin Company, Boston, 1916. (This book was first serialized in the Atlantic Monthly magazine, and Rihbany, himself a Syrina, offers it as "an Oriental guide to afford Occidental readers of the Bible a more intimate view of the original intellectual and social environment of this sacred literature.

Rizk, Salom, Syrian Yankee, Doubleday & Company, Garden City, N.Y. 1952. (An autobiographical account of the Syrian immigrant who told his story to over a million American high school students in the 1940's).

Sengstock, Mary C., "Telkeif, Baghadad, Detroit - Chaldeans Blend Three Cultures, "Michigan History, Volume 54, 1970.

Shadid, Michael A., Crusading Doctor, Meador Publishing Company, Boston, 1956. (The Autobiography of the Arab-American doctor who began the cooperative medicine movement in the United States.)

Suleiman, Michael W., "The New Arab-American Community," in Hagopian and Paden, op. cit., 1969.

The Syrian and Lebanese Texans, Published by the Institute of Texan Cultures, P.O. Box 1226, San Antonio, Texas 78294.

Thabit, Shukrie, My favorite Furnished Room Stories,Thabit Management Company, Brooklyn, New York, 1975. (Humurous accounts of an immigrant Lebanese lady who succeeds brilliantly in the "furnished room" business.)

Wolf, C. Umhau, "Muslims in the American Mid-West," The Muslim World, January, 1960.

Younis, Adele, "The Arabs Who Followed Columbus" Yearbook 1965-66, The Action Committee on American-Arab Relations", New York, 1966.

_____. "The Coming of the Arabic-Speaking People to the United States", unpublished Ph. D. dissertation, Boston University, 1961. (An excellent source of information on those Arab-Americans who arrived before 1961.)